"STEP RIGHT UP, FOLKS!"

"STEP RIGHT UP, FOLKS!"

AL GRIFFIN

Henry Regnery Company · Chicago

[C 1974]

Library of Congress Cataloging in Publication Data

Griffin, Al.
 "Step right up, folks!"

  1. Amusement parks—History, 2. Amusement parks—
Directories. I. Title.
GV1851.G74   1974   791'.068'73   73–19842

Manufactured in the United States of America
International Standard Book Number: 0–8092–9035–9
Library of Congress Catalog Card Number: 73–19842

CONTENTS

PREFACE

Being in love with an amusement park is like loving a woman with a broken nose. You tend to make light of imperfections in your scale of appreciation and come to consider them as part of the charm.

My amusement park was Riverview in Chicago. I was a merry-go-round buff by the age of four. The Fish Tank was robbing me steadily by the time I was six. By eight, I was tall enough to reach the shooting gallery counter, though I *knew* that the rifle sights were so out of line that the only way to win a kewpie doll was by luck. When I was in fifth grade, I held hands with a girl in the Tunnel of Love. And the Bobs was *certainly* the biggest roller coaster in the world, in memory if not in fact.

My first panoramic view of Chicago's northwest side was from a bosun's chair being pulled to the top of the Pair-O-Chutes tower, 225 feet up, with nothing under my feet but space. When I approached the top and looked down, as from the top of a 20-story office building, I gulped to keep from getting dizzy; and between the time I precipitously dropped and the silk chute above me ultimately opened, I *knew* I was done for. Finally, when I

vii

stopped bouncing against the tension springs at the bottom, it was all I could do to swagger back to the crowd of admiring spectators on the ground. Heady stuff.

During high school vacations I worked at Riverview spearing gum wrappers as a clean-up man, making cotton candy, and, for a couple of terrible weeks, manning the Bozo tank. I spent everything I made on the rides and at the hanky-panks. I was a clown in the Mardi Gras parades as Labor Day approached.

Even when I worked, the glamor never lost its glitter. Cheap, tawdry, not-quite-honest, it was still that most fascinating of all entertainment—the traditional amusement park. Since then I have frequented amusement parks all over the country, but in my eyes none ever matched Riverview. Maybe because it is gone now, everything looks better in retrospect.

One day I got an assignment to do a feature article for a magazine about what happened to Riverview's great merry-go-round after the park was razed. Naturally, I jumped at the chance. I tracked the silent merry-go-round to an old warehouse in Galena, Illinois, on the Mississippi River, and from there to a new theme park being built in Georgia. And that set me going.

I haunted historical societies to paw through their old records. Old newspaper files were another source of information I found completely absorbing. Many park operators generously gave me access to their files and records. Not all, though; in such cases I went in undercover to find out what I wanted to know. I ran shooting galleries in Ohio, dealt foot-longs in Texas, repaired roller coasters in California, and was a hat man for the hanky-panks in Florida.

And in all the parks I rode the rides. How I rode! Spending $50 a day at Coney Island was easier than I thought. Some of the machines in the penny arcades in New Jersey take quarters now, but that does not detract from their fascination.

Through it all, as I compiled data for this odyssey of amusement parks, they never lost their gaudy, raucous, decadent enchantment. Naturally, I liked some parks better than others. Some are so pathetically shabby that a visit does not even evoke nostalgia, just an ache. Yet some still evoke the carnie atmosphere of yesteryear. Others are just too dirty, grossly overpriced, or do not have enough variety in rides. But I rated them all (see detailed listings in Section IV), giving 4-star ratings to the great ones down to 1-star ratings for the hopeless ones.

Some amusement parks, indeed, have degenerated into mere kiddielands or theme parks. Though I saw them, I did not rate them (see Section V). As far as I am concerned, a traditional amusement park *has* to have a roller coaster, a *big* merry-go-round, a Ferris wheel, a penny arcade, a shooting gallery, flat rides, a fun house, a dark ride, a midway full of hanky-panks, and picnic facilities. A really good park can get away with not having two or maybe three of these attractions. A fun house, for example, is getting hard to find even in some of the best parks. But I do not consider a porpoise show an amusement park, even if there are picnic facilities on the grounds. Animated statues of comic strip characters and a park landscaped to within an inch of its life does not amuse me either.

It is commonly supposed that the super-sanitized rodents and their followers are taking over the industry. Well, maybe so. There's a lot of money in force-feeding wholesomeness at $5.50 per child, credit cards accepted. Nevertheless the traditional amusement parks are still alive, still the backbone of the industry, which is bigger today than it has ever been. More people will attend amusement parks this year than will attend all professional baseball, football, basketball, and hockey games combined.

There is not yet any need of a requiem for the roller coaster. The Kewpie doll is alive and well and living in Pittsburgh.

March, 1974   Al Griffin

ACKNOWLEDGMENTS

The author is particularly indebted to Irwin Kirby, editor of *Amusement Business,* Nashville, Tennessee, for access to his files going back to the days when the magazine was still called *Billboard.* Many of the photographs in this book are used through the courtesy of that publication.

Numerous historical photographs were also loaned by Jaynie Baker—Belmont Park, San Diego; Roger Conner—Hersheypark, Hershey, Pennsylvania; Robert Garner—Eli Bridge Company, Jacksonville, Illinois; Earl Gascoigne—Geauga Lake Park, Aurora, Ohio; Richard Geist—Playland, Rockaway Beach, New York; Chester Gore—Exhibit Supply Company, Chicago; Darwin Kepler—Conneaut Lake Park, Conneaut Lake, Pennsylvania; and Richard Norton—Lake Compounce, Bristol, Connecticut.

Roberta Friedman, California Institute of the Arts, Valencia, California, and C. W. Osgood, Salem, Oregon, are also owed a debt of gratitude for helping with the illustrations.

The original photography of the eastern seaboard parks was done by Margaret Silinsky.

Especially appreciated was the cooperation of Bob Bell—Bell's Amusement Park, Tulsa, Oklahoma; R. A. Billingsley—Peony Park, Omaha, Nebraska; Bob Blundred—International Association of Amusement Parks, Oak Park, Illinois; Marian Breland—Animal Behavior Enterprises, Hot Springs, Arkansas; Pat Duffy—Idora Park, Youngstown, Ohio; Bo Ekelund—Linnanmäki Amusement Park, Helsinki, Finland; Frederick Fried—New York, New York; Jan Gaski—G&S Amusements, Fountain Valley, California; Jack Gray—Fort Dells, Wisconsin; Carl Hughes—Kennywood Park, West Mifflin, Pennsylvania; Joe Israel—Acme Premium Supply, New York, New York; Ron Knoebel—Knoebel's Groves, Elysburg, Pennsylvania; Bart Kooker—Riverview Park, Des Moines, Iowa; John Kretschmer—Opryland, Nashville, Tennessee; A. E. LaSalle—American Railroad Equipment Association, Irwin, Pennsylvania; George Long—Sea Breeze Amusement Park, Rochester, New York; Howard Lyons—Idlewild Park, Ligonier, Pennsylvania; Joe Maloney—Riverside Park, Agawam, Massachusetts; Roberto Meluzzi—Sarasota, Florida; Francis Messmore—Messmore & Damon, New York, New York; John Miller—Oscar Mayer & Company, Madison, Wisconsin; Stanley Nelson—Joyland, Wichita, Kansas; Robert Ott—Dorney Park, Allentown, Pennsylvania; Fred A. Picard—Geneva, Switzerland; R. Spieldiener—Intamin AG, Zurich, Switzerland; Edgar Streifthau—Fantasy Farm, Middletown, Ohio; Eric Thomas—North American Rides, Montreal, Canada; Aurel Vaszin—National Amusement Device Company, Dayton, Ohio; Michele Walsh—Lusse Brothers, Montgomeryville, Pennsylvania; Nancy Wiley—State Fair of Texas, Dallas; and Bert Williams—Crown Metal Products, Wyano, Pennsylvania.

Plus the hundreds of friends I made on midways all over America.

Part 1

IT'LL NEVER BE THE SAME

1: The Beginnings

THE traction companies that built the first streetcar lines are directly responsible for the development of amusement parks as an American institution.

Some of the most venal robber barons in U.S. history operated most of the car lines, weaseling franchises through bribery in city councils and exacting tolls from carless populations.

The largely uncontrolled syndicates, then operating the electric light and power companies, were no less avaricious, and recognized a good thing when they saw it. In many cases, they charged the traction companies a flat monthly fee for the electricity on which they ran the trolleys, regardless of how much or how little they were used. This irritated the traction magnates because they used hardly any electricity over the weekends. Which is where Yankee ingenuity came into play. The solution to the problem was simply to *make* the public get out and ride the streetcars on Saturdays and Sundays. How? By building an attraction at the end of the car line as a lure to the citizenry.

Starting in New England, the idea spread across the country so quickly that merry-go-round builders were hard put to keep up with the demand for their machines. The idea was a child of the times when there was no television, no movies, no radio, or any other form of inexpensive entertainment. The appeal of picnicking in a shady grove after working in a dingy factory all week, plus the novelty of music and the thrill of rides, made the Sunday trolley excursion almost irresistible. And all the electricity the streetcars used to haul the throngs to the end of the line did not cost the traction company an additional dime. Every nickel that clinked into the fare box was clear profit.

Before long the tail began wagging the dog. Some of the carline executives became so involved in attracting the crowds to the amusement parks that they spent more time building attractions than they spent running the streetcar companies.

For example, the Fitchburg & Leominster Street Railway Company, which built Whalom Park in Lunenburg, Massachusetts, in the late 1890s, was not satisfied with the picnic grove, dance hall, rides, and games on the 75-acre site. By 1900, a 3,000-seat open-sided summer theater was putting on full-scale performances of grand operas (with reserved seats priced at 5¢).*

In Denver, Caruso was a featured attraction at Elitch's Gardens. As soon as the impact of silent movies was felt, amusement parks all over the country were hiring movie stars for personal appearances, including Marie Dressler, Charlie Chaplin, Lillian Gish, Rudolph Valentino, and Theda Bara.

If traction company executives got too caught up in such heady atmospheres, their situation was generally understandable. But not to the stockholders, who soon put a stop to such nonsense. The stockholders could see no point in so rashly spending hundreds of thousands of dollars when, after all, the original purpose of the parks was only to collect those nickel streetcar fares. Once having been built, the parks were serving that purpose regardless of who owned them, and the stockholders insisted that the traction companies sell the parks to private operators and get their money out.

In general, the private purchasers, most of whom had been

---

*Whalom Park is the only amusement park still operated by a street railway company.

squeezed to the last dollar in the selling price by the traction companies, cut many corners in recovering their investments. They
had many reasons for doing so. As in almost any seasonal operation, the owners felt that they had to maintain a policy of "get it
fast while the getting's good." This attitude was intensified in the
amusement business, where the crowds, out to have a good time,
did not worry too much about how much money they were
spending (an attitude that still draws many fast-buck people to
the field). Furthermore, the only buyers many traction companies
could find were those with circus and traveling carnival
backgrounds, some of whom found no novelty in leaving town fast
with the sheriff at their heels.

All these factors added up to a "milking" situation when the
traction companies first pulled out. Unwillingness to invest in
decent maintenance resulted in run-down and even dangerous
equipment. Sometimes the only workers who could be hired for
the wages offered to operate the rides were drunks. Fraudulent
advertising, larcenous games on the midway, and short-changing
the customers were more usual than not. Some parks even sold
exclusive franchises to professional pickpockets. What a way to
run an *amusement* park.

Bilked customers began to complain loudly. Three children
were killed at Coney Island. A delegation of conventioneers in
Chicago were robbed at a Wheel of Fortune game at White City.
In Philadelphia's Woodside Park, a visiting army major from Indianapolis had his wallet lifted by a sexy fortune teller. In
Philadelphia! Things had indeed come to a pretty pass. Local
officials all over the country began getting so many complaints
about undesirable elements in their amusement parks that they
initiated steps to run them out of town.

However, public demand would not allow even the parks
with the worst abuses to close. Amusement parks were still about
the only recreation they had. City fathers tried whole campaigns
of arresting wrongdoers, but there were always more to take their
places. They tried stringent licensing, but their inspectors were
too easy to bribe. A good many politicians finally threw up their
hands and bought out the parks themselves so there might be
greater control.

Geauga Lake in Aurora, Ohio, had one of the longest roller coasters ever built. This photo was taken in 1927.

In the early 1880s, James Parker found that opening his apple orchard to picnickers was more profitable than harvesting apples. He built several buildings on his grounds, including a dance hall that was the fore-runner of Coney Island's Moonlite Gardens.

One of the many attractions at the early Hershey Park was its unique "open front" miniature train.

Cities that still own and operate their own amusement parks today include Chattanooga, Tennessee (Warner Park); Findlay, Ohio (Riverside Amusement Park); Green Bay, Wisconsin (Bay Beach Park); Knoxville, Tennessee (Chilhowee Park); Lafayette, Indiana (Columbian Park); Memphis, Tennessee (Fairgrounds Amusement Park); Paris, Illinois (Twin Lakes Amusement Park); and Providence, Rhode Island (Roger Williams Park). These are all full-scale amusement parks and do not include the many zoos, swimming pools, and beaches run by cities and their park districts where a few kiddie rides and refreshment stands are often a part of the operation. Other cities own the amusement park property but lease it out for operation, such as Elmira, New York, where Eldridge Park is one of the best-run major amusement parks in the country today.

Sometimes, in the bad old days, where municipalities were unable to do so, county governments moved in to control parks as their own property. Amusement parks still owned and operated by county governments include Lakemont Amusement Park in Altoona, Pennsylvania (Blair County); Hart Memorial Park in Bakersfield, California (Kern County); Neptune Amusement Park, St. Simon's Island, Georgia (Glynn County); and Westchester County's aging but still great Playland Amusement Park in Rye, New York, where the ice rink is a famous summer favorite.

Civic-minded groups who did the same thing on their own, and still operate parks today as their own property, include the Chamber of Commerce in Jacksonville, Florida (Boardwalk Beach Amusement Park); City Merchants Association in Salem, Massachusetts (Salem Willows Park); and even a group headed by the Reverend Ivan Dornick in Uniontown, Pennsylvania, who is now the outright nominal owner of Shady Grove Amusement Park. For a while, service organizations such as the Kiwanis, Rotary, and Lions Clubs ran amusement parks. The American Legion was in the business, too, but the last two parks they owned and operated were Lake Cisco Amusement Park in Cisco, Texas, and American Legion Park in Hawthorne, Pennsylvania, both of which folded in 1972.

As the parks evolved into big business in the early twentieth century, they attracted more respectable management. A park with a major investment in large parcels of real estate, dozens of permanent rides, restaurants, ballrooms, skating rinks, concert halls, and elaborate picnic and boating facilities was not about to allow some grifter to shortchange a Girl Scout or bring the kind of heat that could pull its expensive reputation down around its ears. High finance likes repeat business, and solid citizens moved into the industry. Forest Park, the huge amusement complex in St. Louis, Missouri, was built by a brewery. So was Pabst Park in Milwaukee, Wisconsin. Showman George Hamid's Steel Pier in Atlantic City, New Jersey, helped change the whole image of amusement parks. In Chicago, Bill Schmidt, the son of a wealthy real estate man, built massive Riverview Park after coming home from a trip to Europe, where he had been impressed by such jewels as Tivoli Gardens in Copenhagen, Denmark, where amusement parks had been in business as beer gardens long before Sam Yerkes ever thought of going into the streetcar business.

Another feature copied from Europe was the resort. America's resort areas and bathing pavilions go far back, but they were for the relatively well-to-do and were few in number before the streetcar companies came along.

Lake Compounce in Bristol, Connecticut, is America's oldest amusement park in continuous operation under the same management, having celebrated its 128th season in 1973. Even before Gad Norton organized it as a commercial bathing beach and concert grove in 1846, Lake Compounce had been in use by the Norton family for personal summer recreation since the area had been acquired from the Indians in 1684. The original deed, written in Old English script, bears the marks of several Tunxis Indians along with that of their leader, Chief Compound, listed first.

The deed transferred the title to the early English settlers known as The 84 Proprietors, one of whom, John Norton, was one of Gad Norton's forefathers. It is not known what Chief Compound thought he was getting out of the deal, but John Norton may well have been the first to say, "I'll tell ya what I'm gonna do . . ." in a long line of spielers on the same ground that is now the midway under the roller coasters at Lake Compounce (they didn't even get the poor Indian's name spelled correctly). The amusement park is still owned and operated by the Norton family.

While Lake Compounce was built for people with their own transportation, Vauxhall Gardens, built in what is now New York's Bowery, was for those who had none. Its proprietors liked the name because there was a famous Vauxhall Gardens in Paris, the name of which had in turn been stolen from the first internationally famous amusement resort of all—Vauxhall Gardens in London, which had been built almost 200 years before the New Yorkers built theirs in the 1850s.

Jones Wood was another early amusement park in Manhattan, a 150-acre tract on the East River in what is now the area of high-rises between 70th and 75th streets. Patrons enjoyed lodge outings, political rallies, beer drinking, and shooting contests (which have since moved over to Central Park). Such places, however, were not much favored by families who had the means of transportation to get out of town.

Instead, they went to new resorts. Long Branch, New Jersey, 30 miles south of New York City, was the first of many bathing resorts to be built in the 1850s and 1860s. From this nucleus, a string of summer amusement parks finally extended down the Jersey seacoast past Atlantic City all the way to Wildwood at the foot of the peninsula.

Cincinnati's swells rode chartered steamboats twenty miles along the Ohio River to reach Parker's Island, a converted apple orchard featuring a dance hall, bowling alley, shooting gallery, and mule-powered merry-go-round. In 1883 the grove was taken over by new management and reorganized as a full-scale amusement park called Ohio Grove, the Coney Island of the West, and the Midwest Coney Island grew to be the best-managed amusement park in the entire country.

With Coney Island operating the largest and most elaborate excursion steamer in the world, patrons no longer had to charter their own boats. After a quarter of a century of magnificent service, the original million-dollar *Island Queen* blew up at its Pittsburgh dock. But it was only one of the many *Island Queen* excursion boats being operated by Coney Island; in all, there have been 19 of them operated by the amusement park.

Many early amusement parks were built around a single attraction, such as a Ferris wheel in a vacant lot, a miniature railroad (especially if it was steam), or even a roller coaster built by people who just liked roller coasters, as at Columbia Gardens in Butte, Montana. Columbia added a flying swing and a small merry-go-round as a sop to the patronage, but it was known as Roller Coaster Park as long as it lasted.

Geauga Lake Park in Aurora, Ohio, is another amusement park started by roller coaster buffs. By 1927 that park boasted one of the longest such rides in the world. At the foot of the start-peak of the roller coaster, Geauga also had one of the biggest swimming pools ever built anywhere, which proved to be so popular that the cost was 10¢ just to get close enough to look.

Dreamland Park (Sea Breeze) in Rochester, New York, was finally and permanently acquired by George Long, a merry-go-round buff of the first caliber. Previously the park had gone through several ownerships following a start as an electric trolley park when Long was just a kid. To this day he still carves merry-go-round horses.

Hershey Park in Hershey, Pennsylvania, was built around a Hershey Chocolate Bar, not rides. The company was delighted to open a picnic grounds where everybody was encouraged to have one of their confections for dessert. Because swimming uses up a lot of sugar energy, Hershey lost no time in building one of the biggest pools in Pennsylvania. It had the highest and longest slide into the water ever built anywhere. Hershey also offered canoeing as another healthful exercise.

Their unique miniature railroad was another big attraction, with the engineer sitting at the controls in the middle of the train instead of at the front. This allowed patrons to sit in the open for an unobstructed view of the gardens. To attract the even larger crowds, Hershey built a bandstand where some of the biggest names in music, drama, and vaudeville performed. The outdoor concerts were free, although Hershey paid lavishly for the talent they wanted.

Hershey was also a pioneer in the development of what came to be known as kiddielands. In 1915 a corner of the grounds was set aside for some ordinary slides and swings, as in any playground. By the end of World War I, however, they had a kids' dry-land "boat ride"—each bathtub-sized car accommodated two preschoolers under a striped canopy and undulated gently up and down as it went around a circular wooden track. In the 1920s a kid-sized Ferris wheel had 'em waiting in line for a 5¢ ride in one of the completely caged cars that rose to a height of 18 feet. The kids were sophisticated enough by the 1930s to tool around a scaled-down race track in self-powered and well-bumpered electric cars.

Interestingly enough, the original amusement parks were basically designed for adults, not for children. The transition was spurred by the immensely successful diverse development of the most famous name in amusement park history—Coney Island.

The popular legend has it that Coney Island is an amusement park like the one in any hometown, only bigger. Not so. Coney Island is simply another geographical location in New York, like Staten Island or Manhattan Island. It is a sand pit with good swimming at the lower end of Brooklyn, where a great number of individual amusement enterprises are operated. The famous old Cyclone roller coaster, for example, was a singly owned attraction.

The nucleus around which all the other Coney Island attractions grew was Sea Lion Park, founded by the self-styled Captain Billy Boyton in 1895. Boyton was one of the most colorful characters ever to get into the business. While he was a lifeguard at Atlantic City, he got involved in a scheme to promote a lifesaving invention for timid ocean travelers. It was a rubber suit with five vulcanized air chambers that, when inflated, allowed the wearer to float in either an upright or a recumbent position so he could paddle along or rest. The idea was to rent these outfits to transatlantic passengers, and Boyton's brainstorm was to publicize the suit by jumping off a Europe-bound steamer when it was 200 miles out of New York and then paddling back home.

Boyton's announcement of the plan to the newspapers alerted all the ship captains. Thus, though he managed to sneak aboard the steamer *Queen* with his contraption on October 11, 1874, he was caught on the second day out as he was getting ready to jump. His rig was confiscated to prevent any further foolhardy attempts, and he was locked in his cabin for good measure. But he successfully pleaded with the captain to let him complete the experiment, and on October 21, he was dropped over the side in his rubber suit off the Irish coast.

He made it to shore. Boyton proceeded to give exhibitions in rivers all over Europe, and by the time he got back to the United States he was famous. He demonstrated his remarkable suit in a swim down the Mississippi River from Alton, Illinois, to St. Louis, Missouri, and subsequently in other waterways all over America. The trouble was that nobody rented any suits. So this inventive publicist assembled a big water circus and, after touring the country with his show, settled in the meadows of South Brooklyn with the show because it was close to many potential customers and the real estate was cheap.

Boyton called it Sea Lion Park and began to try to make money. At first, he was unsuccesful. His 40 trained seals failed to attract enough people with their juggling act. Next, Boyton built the first large-scale Shoot-the-Chutes in America, and suddenly he was in the amusement park business. Unfortunately, he was not a success. Though he might have understood lifesaving (doubtful), he never understood the amusement park business, and after he had spent a small fortune building a big ballroom, in 1899, where few people ever danced, his shaky operation was taken over by Thompson and Dundy.

This pair was as unlikely as Boyton to succeed in the amusement park business. Elmer Dundy was an Omaha politician, and Fred Thompson was a Tennessee tinker. When Thompson was 24 years old, he got a job building components for the Tennessee State Fair. The fair was a financial flop, and when Thompson was unable to collect his fee, he accepted one of the exposition buildings instead.

In 1898 he tried to enter the Omaha Exposition with it and was dismayed to find that a local man had already applied for a similar concession. Right: it was Dundy, who had enough political clout as clerk of the United States Court in Omaha to get the concession Thompson wanted. However, Elmer had sufficient brains to realize that the newcomer from Tennessee had the better attraction, so they pooled their meager resources—with such results that Dundy quit his job to work with Thompson full-time. After a successful run at the Pan-American Exposition in Buffalo, New York, they took an illusion concession called A Trip to the Moon to Coney Island, where they set up shop in 1902 at Boyton's new competition, Tilyou's Steeplechase Park.

When they heard that Boyton was going broke, the two tyros bought out Sea Lion Park so they could try out a new idea—installation of a midway similar to the one that had become so famous at the Chicago Columbian Exposition. The remodeling was handled personally by Fred Thompson, who had no sense of the value of money and who utterly disregarded costs. His partner tried as well as he could to keep expenditures in line, but Thompson and Dundy not only spent all the cash they could raise for construction but completely exhausted their credit as well.

By opening day, May 16, 1903, they were down to $22—barely enough for change for the ticket booths. At eight o'clock that night, the 250,000 electric lights Thompson had had installed were switched on and the 5-lane gate was thrown open. By 10:30, over 40,000 people had crowded in at a dime per head. The major attractions they were privileged to patronize included the remodeled Shoot-the-Chutes, an Old Mill, Miniature Railway, Hagenbeck's Wild Animal Show, Canals of Venice, Dragon's Gorge, Monkey Theater, Grand Ballroom, German Village, Eskimo Village, Electric Tower, Infant Incubator, Trip to the North Pole, and War of the Worlds.

The bachelor partners, who had never forgotten their successful concession at the Buffalo Exposition, called the new Coney Island operation Luna Park. It was so successful that it was a major influence all over the world before World War I. There still are amusement parks called Luna Park in Melbourne and Sydney, Australia (where hot-dogs are called Coney Islands). Thompson and Dundy had finally hit it big—without really knowing what they were doing.

These two one-time amateurs thereupon proceeded to expand operations by going into something else they knew nothing about —bigtime show business. With the help of John "Bet-a-Million"

Gates, they built the New York Hippodrome, a $4 million building, designed by Thompson, occupying the entire block on the east side of 6th Avenue between 43rd and 44th Streets with seats for over 6,000 people. Here they produced costly spectaculars combining the best circus and stage acts, of a magnitude that outdid anything else ever produced before or since.

Unfortunately, Dundy died in 1907, leaving the profligate Fred Thompson unchecked. He bought yachts, married an actress, and starred her in a succession of costly Broadway plays. By 1908 he had lost the Hippodrome to the Shuberts, and his growing list of creditors took over Luna Park in 1912. His last shot was a flop called A Grand Toyland at the San Francisco Exposition, and he died bankrupt in New York in 1919 at the age of 46. The by-then decrepit Luna Park itself burned down during World War II.

Coney Island's famous Dreamland Park was built in 1904 on the heels of Luna Park's fabulous success and cost $3.5 million. As a good start, Dreamland's promoters pirated Luna's best-grossing attractions, including even their Infant Incubator (an exhibit of newborn infants under the care of a corps of trained nurses, amusement-park style).

Dreamland extended all the way from Surf Avenue to the beach and included one of the ocean piers, on which the promoter built the biggest ballroom in the world. A double-runway Shoot-the-Chutes extended all the way out over the ocean. The Lilliputian Village had a resident population of some 300 midgets; a scenic railway had jingling sleighs coasting over snow-covered Alps against a vast Swiss panorama; gondolas floated serenely through the Canals of Venice; and a 300-foot Tower of Seville (bigger than Luna's tower) rose majestically from the center of the illuminated lagoon.

Dreamland was known as the Gibraltar of the amusement world. The management lined up theatrical stars by the dozen. Mostly for the publicity, they got Marie Dressler to invest in the peanut and popcorn concession, and she promptly dressed up her young lady vendors in a 1908 version of Bunny costumes. But the most exciting show in the park was an illusion called Fighting Flames, where a full-sized 6-story building was set on fire every night; clanging fire engines and thrilling rescues held the crowds enthralled. Schoolteachers brought entire classes to see the spectacle. Fighting Flames inspired hundreds of New York kids to become firemen.

By this time, Coney Island had so many different operations competing with each other that some entrepreneurs began capitalizing on the fact that many families were bringing their children to see the sights. A go-getter by the name of Eugene Silinsky installed the nation's first "petting zoo" to attract families to his Edinburgh Gardens amusement park. An imaginative young man by the name of John Mertes, a bit ahead of this time (1910) built a ¼ acre playground with sandboxes, slides, and regulation swings for children—a combination forerunner of today's one-price policies and baby-sitting services—and began to get rich on his 10¢ admissions.

Seeing all this, a delegation of executives from Kennywood Park, the old Mellon trolley park outside Pittsburgh, went home to build the first true kiddieland. Using the big park's 16 most popular rides as models, they scaled-down the amusement devices to moppet size and did so much business the first season that they had to expand the kiddieland the following year. In its heyday, Kennywood's kiddieland was an inspiration for American amusement parks all over the country.

But all the kids grew up.

2: Beginning of the End

THINGS changed after World War II. For one thing, returning servicemen were too sophisticated still to find satisfactory the simple amusements young men formerly had found more than adequate. They, and the rest of America, wanted more action, and the amusement parks were not supplying it. The park owners tried. A dark ride known as The Mill on the Floss—a leisurely passage through man-made caverns in boats floating in a machine-driven current—was summarily renamed The Tunnel of Love at Palisades Park in New Jersey. The pattern was followed by about everybody else in the country, but that was hardly enough for the jaded United States.

In Chicago, Riverview's air jets in the Fun House, which blew up a girl's dress so ogling spectators could get a tantalizing glimpse of her pants, titillated for only a short while. Most all girls not only wear slacks today, but everybody knows what's under them. The girls quit riding Riverview's merry-go-round horses sidesaddle long before that park closed. Riverview's 225-foot parachute drop was the talk of the industry when it was built in 1937, but it held little awe for a GI who had been dropped over France in a real parachute.

Many eastern parks, in particular—among them Rainbow Gardens in McKeesport, Pennsylvania, and Carrousel Gardens just outside Buffalo, New York—closed because their patronage had grown too sophisticated for what they offered. But the worst example of a park management's underestimation of the market's sophistication was a more recent undertaking, Freedomland, in Queens in New York City. The massive park, built in the shape of the U.S. territorial outline, featured regional shows in appropriate geographical sections along with rides, games, and everything else that should appeal to merrymakers—in Des Moines, maybe. Nobody has yet figured out why promoter Bill Zeckendorf thought such a yokel operation could compete in New York City with Times Square, the Empire State Building, the Statue of Liberty, Rockefeller Center, the United Nations Building, Greenwich Village, Fifth Avenue, the Bronx Zoo, great museums all over the city, Radio City Music Hall, *all* the major legitimate theaters, and first-run movies always premiering in New York.

Even spending another $250,000 for one of the finest antique merry-go-rounds in the world could not pull the $30 million investment out of the hole, and the promoters resorted to such desperation moves as installing a coterie of Greek belly dancers and Roman Chariot Races, a wax museum featuring the Last Supper, tableaus of King Arthur's Knights, the Three Musketeers, Charge of the Light Brigade, and the Bengal Lancers; and other such inappropriate attractions for Freedomland U.S.A. The midway became a hive of the worst kind of blatant merchandising.

As any pretense of good taste disappeared, so did any remnants of serious patronage. Freedomland wound up a financial debacle. Bill Zeckendorf was a wizard in the field of housing and industrial construction. He should have stuck to that instead of branching out into something that was over his head. Many parks have gone out of business because their original appeal could no longer hold an increasingly sophisticated market. Freedomland went broke because its original appeal never existed.

A startling number of amusement parks no longer in business did not go broke—they burned down. Flimsy construction, careless precautions, and poor fire-fighting equipment have resulted in the destruction of dozens of them. Disastrous fires have been particularly hard on Coney Island. In 1907, a $1 million fire burned out Steeplechase Park, although George Tilyou rebuilt it "greater than ever." Even worse was the total destruction of Dreamland Park as it was being readied for the 1911 season—a $5 million wipe-out.

Despite legend, Dreamland's 1911 debacle did not start at the Fighting Flames attraction (see Chapter 10). It broke out after an overheated tar pot set fire to a building called Hell Gate. Unfortunately, the Fighting Flames firemen were actors, not bona fide fire fighters. The entire park was in flames before the Brooklyn firemen could reach the scene. A double triple-alarm brought firefighting apparatus from every part of the burrough and from New York City itself. As many as 45 fire companies fought the conflagration, but even fire boats brought up to the beach could not help. Dreamland burned to the ground and was never rebuilt.

The fire that permanently put Luna Park out of business burned down more than half of the 40 acres Thompson and Dundy had built up some 40 years before. After the remaining rides were dismantled, the area was covered with debris for years. It was cleared finally in 1949—for a parking lot.

The only major fire on record in which arson is suspected is the fire that burned down Paradise Park in Rye, New York, in the 1920s, after Westchester County officials forced out the rascals who had been running it. Before the county could take over the operation themselves as an on-the-level enterprise as planned, the place "mysteriously" burned to the ground in the dead of night. Westchester County reopened it as Playland Park in 1928, just one year before the Great Depression hit, and made the politicians wish they had left matters to take care of themselves.

Much of the equipment destroyed in amusement park fires can never be replaced. One of the only four 5-abreast merry-go-rounds ever built, for example, was lost in the 1912 fire at Ocean Park in Los Angeles. Five other Philadelphia Toboggan antique merry-go-rounds (see Chapter 3) were destroyed by fires in Detroit, Michigan; Chattanooga, Tennessee; Wildwood, New Jersey; Flint, Michigan; and Nantasket Beach, Massachusetts.

Natural disasters also take their toll of amusement parks.

Forest Park in St. Louis, Missouri, a favorite picnic grove and
beer garden during the 1890s, was leveled by an 1896 cyclone. Its
operators owed a $10,000 beer bill they could not pay, so the
Home Brewing Company settled for ownership of the park.
Subsequent installation of rides, a bandstand, and a summer theater made it one of the great amusement parks of the Midwest.

Floods have always been a hazard to parks built along river
banks. The rampageous Ohio River has inundated Cincinnati's
Coney Island with spring floods many times, once to a depth of 52
feet. Coney Island is gone for good now, but not just because of
the floods. In fact, they account for one reason why the Cincy
Coney has always been such an excellent park; the equipment
never even got a chance to get old, as in so many other slowly rot-
ting amusement parks. After each flood, the Ohio Coney Island
was refurbished with extensive repairs and rebuilding, so that it
was always one of the most up-to-date parks in America.

The venerable Luna Park decayed through sheer negligence
before it mercifully burned down. After Fred Thompson lost it,
his successors failed to continue its profitable operation. Season
after season, Luna Park was operated without adding any new attractions, and existing ones were run without proper maintenance
until they simply fell apart. Patronage petered out accordingly,
and for years the forlorn derelict park stood entirely idle.

Amusement areas that are part of an amusement complex—for
example, Coney Island in Brooklyn—and are allowed to die an un-
dignified death are so depressing that they affect the other amusement operations around them. The Wonder Wheel recognized no
competition when it was built as the most spectacular Ferris
wheel in the world. Taller than a 20-story building, it had a separate wheel within the outer wheel, and the cars slid between the
two wheels by gravity on this super-scary ride. But by 1962, its
defunct neighbors were under the wrecker's demolition hammer.
The scene around the Wonder Wheel was just too depressing to
attract enough merrymakers to keep it a paying proposition, until
the demolished site became today's $3 million Astroland.

Palisades Park's dismal penny arcade certainly did not do
much to prevent the demise of that institution; nor did its Wild

Mouse, the jerk-back coaster, which was never smoothed out even after most of its dazed patrons concluded that it was just too bone-jarring to ride a second time.

Some parks obstinately kept right on running old rides after they were hopelessly out of date. Fairyland Park in Oakland, California, ran a miniature railroad modeled after the Toonerville Trolley comic strip long after the day when potential riders could feel any nostalgia. Whittington Park in Hot Springs, Arkansas, had rides based on old comic-strip characters nobody under 30 had ever heard of. Other parks that passed on because they simply got out of date include Hanson's Amusement Park in Harvey's Lake, Pennsylvania; Playland Park, Council Bluffs, Iowa; Washington Park, El Paso, Texas; and Jantzen Beach Park, Portland, Oregon.

Some parks willing to make changes made the wrong changes. Swope Park in Kansas City, Missouri, thought they would have a winner with their Zoo Ride—a merry-go-round with lions, camels, greyhounds, and other exotic animals, instead of the traditional horses. Like housewives asked to buy salt in square boxes, nobody went near the idea.

Pure and simple competition has put few parks out of business, at least not within the industry itself. Television has closed no amusement parks; going to an amusement park is too much of a special occasion. The advent of movies had more of an effect. The old Forest Park Highlands, for example, at one time put on the best shows in St. Louis, featuring top vaudeville acts, Sousa's band, and celebrities such as Jack Dempsey, but dropped the policy in 1920 in the face of competition from the motion-picture industry. Perhaps Playland Park in Houston, Texas, is the closest to the exemplary park that fell victim to industry competition. It simply could not compete with the huge new Astroworld amusement complex.

Astroworld itself is in deep trouble, and it would not be the first park to find itself too big for its economic britches. Pacific Ocean Park in Santa Monica, California, built 40 major rides and attractions (Cincinnati's Coney Island had 19), 20 refreshment stands, and half a dozen full-fledged restaurants, plus twice as much of everything else than anybody used. The huge park could never generate enough midway traffic to support such a vast operation.

Of course, that is only one person's opinion. Among those who disagree is Dick Geist, the outspoken operator of the legendary Playland at Rockaway Beach, New York. "Their pay-one-price policy is what did 'em in," he insists. "The few dollars paid at the gate covered every ride in the park. And the customer who came in as the gates opened in the morning could ride as many times as he wanted to, on anything he liked, until closing time at night. There just was no way to cover their kind of multi-million dollar investment with a pay-one-price policy. And on good days when big crowds did show up, they wore out the equipment on popular rides without anybody paying for its repair and replacement."

Geist is understandably biased because on Saturday night he gets $1 per ride on his roller coaster, with the rest of Rockaway's Playland priced accordingly. But the P.O.P. policy used in Santa Monica was nothing new in the industry, having been used by George Tilyou at Steeplechase Park as early as 1903. Moreover, most of the successful theme parks (see Part V) use a one-price policy, too.

Theme parks also use another gimmick few traditional parks have been able to get away with—over-commercialization. Few things will turn-off a customer as much as spending a lot of money and then being hammered with commercials from participating sponsors. This was one of the many sins committed by Palisades Park, which used promotional tie-ins more than any other traditional park in the country.

Palisades would both name a ride after practically any product or company that would come up with a $6,000 fee and distribute 35,000 samples of the product to the patrons as well as plug the product or sponsor in any way possible. In 1969 the captive audience was subjected to such promotions as Coca Cola's Hi-C, Pepsi-Cola's Mountain Dew, Philip Morris' Clark gum, Luden's mint candies, Proctor & Gamble's Top Job cleaner and Prell Concentrate, Hormel's Spam, General Foods' Maxwell House coffee, and Quaker Oats' Cap'n Crunch cereal.

Palisades had always been strong on talent shows, and all of a sudden there was Miss Teenage America sipping a can of Hi-C.

There was a Ken-L-Ration Dog Show and a particularly ob-
noxious Mountain Dew Country Music Talent Show. The Sky
Ride became the Top Job Sky Ride, the Cyclone became the
Clark Gum Cyclone, the mery-go-round became the Cosmetically
Yours Carousel, and the restaurant became the Maxwell Coffee
House. They even sold television rights to a local station for cov-
erage of their roller coaster. That kind of thing might be accepted
at a World's Fair but not at an amusement park.

At the time, of course, Palisades Park was literally fighting for
its life. However, every $6,000 fee taken in simply prolonged the
closing a little longer.

What finally did in Palisades was the loss of the bulk of its
traditional market to that bane of most inner-city amusement
parks—vandalism. The relaxed atmosphere under which most
traditional amusement parks operate can be completely misun-
derstood. Though amusement parks have always had to cope with
sailors on leave, college kids full of beer, high school punks, and
other rowdies, today's bewildered, unemployed hoodlum is likely
to vandalize anything to compensate for his sense of inferiority.
Vandalism has doomed more amusement parks than any other
single factor.

Washington, D.C., has the biggest proportion of inner-city
poor of any comparable city in the country. Indeed, the Washington poor are so numerous that they could have turned Glen Echo
Park, 12 miles outside the city, into a park of their own, as have
Chicago's South Side kids with Funtown Amusement Park on
95th Street. Instead, the Washington gangs destroyed Glen Echo.

Glen Echo had an illustrious history. The 20-acre tract was
developed in 1883 as a branch settlement of the national Chautauqua educational and religious movement, which had started in
upstate New York. The biggest building, which once boasted the
largest and most magnificent organ in North America, was converted to a fun house when the property was acquired by the
street railway company in 1889 and made into an amusement
park. Subsequently, new owners, who took over the park in 1911,
built up Glen Echo to be one of the most successful operations in
the United States.

The Ohio River destroyed Cincinnati's Coney Island in 1964.

Demolition work at New York's Coney Island, May, 1962.

A victim of man's own greed, Freedomland degenerated into catch-penny poor taste.

Riverview's Pair-O-Chutes was a sensation — in 1937.

That was a long time ago. In its last days, Glen Echo was simply a dangerous place to visit. Gangs of young hoodlums sometimes stood under the Alpine Sky Ride and pelted its helpless passengers overhead with beer cans and pop bottles. One youth was shot down with a steel ball bearing from a slingshot as he swung by like a duck in a shooting gallery. Women were molested constantly; fights raged almost every weekend; and concessionaires were robbed left and right. The park was in shambles by the time it finally closed down.

Dark rides have been closed down all over the country because of muggings therein. Rape in the fun house is not funny. Openly taking a leak behind the merry-go-round is more than just bad manners. All too often, faced with such affronts, people with money to spend just stopped going to once-great amusement parks—as was the case at Fontainne Ferry Park in Louisville, Kentucky.

Robbing concessions at Riverside Park in Indianapolis, Indiana, was standard procedure; while two kids started a simulated fight to distract the attendant, a third vaulted over the counter and rifled the cash box. At Euclid Beach Park in Cleveland, Ohio, gangs would simply rush a popcorn stand for whatever money they could pick up out of the debris.

Penny arcades are particularly hard hit. At old Riverview in Chicago, half a dozen kids would crowd around a machine so that passersby could not see that one was breaking open the cash box. Smashing an irreplaceable antique machine meant nothing to punks intent on stealing only a handful of coins. Dozens of machines were sometimes wrecked in a single night. Crystal Beach Park in Canada, across from Buffalo, New York, has an even worse problem than most parks in that any U.S. culprit arrested and released on bond has to be extradited from the United States for prosecution.

All existing parks in metropolitan areas maintain expensive security systems, with varying degrees of effectiveness. Most of them publicly deny that they have any special security problems. Dick Geist, of Rockaway's Playland, is one of those who pooh-pooh the idea. However, he has erected cyclone fences 20-feet high around his properties.

One park, which shall here be nameless, became particularly disgusted with the red tape involved in prosecuting vandals and with judges merely giving a slap on the wrist. In addition to the regular security force, the park hired an unofficial muscle squad of ex-boxers and football players who never bothered to arrest anyone. When anybody gets out of line, the plug-ugglies summarily drag him out to the parking lot and beat him up. Few complaints have been filed, and when the police come around to investigate, the manager simply points to the uniformed college boys who comprise his official security force. The word has gotten around town, and although gate traffic has dropped off in hoodlum patronage, dollar volume is up as customers, people looking for fun instead of trouble, are returning to the park.

Still other parks ceased operation when the cities grew up too rapidly around them, and traffic problems became too much for potential patrons. One of Pacific Palisades' many problems was that it was increasingly hard to get to in the later years. Getting out, especially after a big show or a holiday that had drawn large crowds, could be an unbelievably difficult matter at closing time. Cincinnati's Coney Island unsuccessfully battled the same situation for years. So did Wedgewood Park in Oklahoma City and Sans Souci Park in Wilkes-Barre, Pennsylvania, before they went out of business.

The cities' inexorable appetite for prime land has put many parks out of business as developers gobbled up the parks' real estate for housing and industrial developments. For example, the property at Funtown in Atlanta, Georgia, just became too valuable. As the city closed in around it, there simply was no room for the acreage needed to run a decent-sized miniature railroad. Forest Park in Hanover, Pennsylvania, succumbed to pressure from the city planners; Olympic Park in Mapleton-Irving, New Jersey, went the same way; and even the great Savin Rock Park in West Haven, Connecticut, "got an offer they couldn't refuse."

But amusement park owners are a breed of men apart, and many are not even in the business just for the money. Most major parks have been owned by the same families for generations. The

closed-ranks attitude of long-established amusement park operators is unique. Say a tornado wrecks an amusement park —
equipment and technicians are flown in from parks all over the
country with no questions asked about credit, and sometimes
even before help is asked for.

Part of this camaraderie may stem from the fact that major
amusement parks do not directly compete with each other; each
usually has a separate geographical territory. More likely, the
owners' solidarity is due to a mutual sense that they are all threat-
ened by the many forces beyond their control.

And there is not much doubt about it—operators of traditional
amusement parks are an endangered species. The statistics, found
in the appendix, are too grim not to be taken seriously.

Part 2

THE RIDES

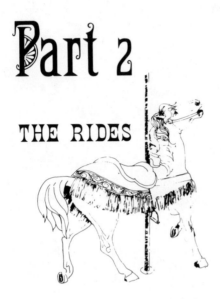

3: Merry-Go-Rounds

GEORGE Geist likes to say, "The world's most beautiful music is the sound of children's laughter." In fact, with all apple pie and motherhood aside, to the people of the park, the world's most beautiful music is the sound of whirring turnstiles at the entry gate—with one possible exception: merry-go-round music.

A carrousel in France and a roundabout in England, it is a merry-go-round in the United States. And in many ways the merry-go-round is exceptional. For a start it is the only exception to the assumption that all traditional amusement park rides are for grown-ups. As the ringmaster at the circus says, "It's for children of all ages."

The merry-go-round's appeal is truly universal. It's for toddlers who glory in riding with the big kids. It's for preschoolers who get a rapturous chance to prove themselves. "You don't have to hold me on, Ma!" has been heard on every merry-go-round in the world. It's for young daredevils in dream worlds who think of themselves as cowboys, knights, and sultans on their prancing steeds. A merry-go-round is for exuberant show-offs yelling to their relatives on the sidelines. A merry-go-round is for strivers reaching for the brass ring. A merry-go-round is for radio-raised kids who find out as they whirl around for the first time what music really can be when they hear the tunes of good times swelling from the huge band organ.

Young lovers, proud mothers, and nostalgia buffs are all passionate, sometimes sentimental, fans of the merry-go-round. One old codger who had been bringing his wife to Riverview for many years finally was noticed coming to ride the merry-go-round by himself. For several years he even needed a cane to climb aboard. When the motion of the jumping horses got too much for him, he gravely rode the stationary horses. Bill Schmidt eventually presented him with a lifetime pass, but he outlived the park.

A real merry-go-round buff gets his first ride at around the age of three. The anticipation is almost unbearable as he waits in line, watching and listening to the surge of joy around him. When he is finally lifted onto the enormous horse, he clutches the riser pole as if his young life depended on it. His face assumes expressions of awe, delight, terror, and glee, all at the same time. Trumpets sound and cymbals crash, and slowly, inch-by-inch, the merry-go-round starts to move. The terrible horse under him sinks toward the floor. Then, as it rises majestically, the merry-go-round starts to pick up speed. The music pours over him, and a whole new world of ectasy opens up. Damn!

Very few merry-go-round riders grabbing for the brass ring realize that they are performing an ancient act. Once the brass ring represented serious business, but today it just entitles the triumphant winner to a free ride.

Young nobles and princes 300 years ago practiced tournament jousting with a simple rotating frame on which they could ride while trying to spear a ring with their lances. The Italian word for jousting is *carosello*, a corruption of the diminutive, meaning "quarrelsome." Formal jousting was popular in court circles all over Europe, and Louis XIV staged a tournament in 1662 so elaborate that the Paris site is still called Place du Carrousel, between the Louvre and the Tuileries.

Spelling of the word *carrousel* is moot. Gustav Dentzel, the most famous American merry-go-round builder, spelled it "caroussell" on his shop sign when he opened for business in 1867. On his letterheads, used during the 1880s, he dropped the final *l*. When his son succeeded him, the spelling got back the second *l* and added a second *r* as well. Stein and Goldstein, who built the largest merry-go-rounds ever made, spelled it "carousal"—did they think of it as a matter of "carousing"—in 1914, as did William F. Mangels, a famous inventor, builder, and the industry's historian. Though later he spelled it "carrousel" throughout a book published in 1952.

Frederick Fried spells it "carousel" in his *A Pictorial History of the Carousel*. Gottfried Bungarz, the Brooklyn builder of Coney Island rides, added a final *e* to the word on his nameplates. Even the dictionaries disagree. But the double *r*, as used by Louis XIV, appears generally to be accepted, and, anyway, it seems to give the plebian "merry-go-round" the dignity it deserves.

And to listen to a good many amusement park operators is to be impressed with the antecedents of the merry-go-round: "This isn't an ordinary merry-go-round. It's a genuine carrousel with hand-carved horses made in Germany. Come here and look at the nameplate on the band organ. See? It says right here, 'Made in Berlin.' " Oh, well, it's a good line. In fact, the overwhelming majority of merry-go-rounds that have *ever* been used in the United States have been built right here. Most of the early band *organs*, which were indeed imported from Europe, had names carved on their elaborate facades, but they were merely components. Merry-go-round manufacturing for the U.S. market was strictly a homegrown industry.

The emphasis on German manufacture stems from a single 1911 sensation at Coney Island called El Dorado, which was indeed imported whole from Leipzig, Germany. Over 60 feet in diameter and 40 feet high, it had three tiers of revolving platforms, each running at a different speed. Its band organ was an enormous mass of carved figures, all tapping on glockenspiels, triangles, cymbals, and drums. Its powerful tone reverberated throughout Coney Island. It ran as an independent attraction at 11th and Surf Streets until the Dreamland fire, after which

George Tilyou bought it for Steeplechase Park. With his genius for publicity, Tilyou made El Dorado a national institution, and customers such as Teddy Roosevelt, Enrico Caruso, and Eddie Cantor rode it to help spread its fame.°

Hoping that some of El Dorado's glory would rub off on them, many American merry-go-round operators announced that their machines, too, were German-made. The myths have never died, and today many an amusement park operator himself believes them, though, in fact, the only other major import from Germany known to exist is the carrousel in Nashville, Tennessee, at Opryland. Advertised by the park as being 65 feet in diameter, it actually measures 40 feet across, but nevertheless it is a grand old machine. Dating back to the 1870s, it is one of the oldest operating amusement rides in the world.

The Opryland machine is not, however, a traditional merry-go-round. The eight elaborately carved gondolas resemble horse-drawn carriages, but there are no horses. The entire structure is covered with ornate carvings of German girls, cherubs, and bats (a German good luck symbol). In 1970 Pete Logan, of Showcrafts, Inc., Miami, Florida, found it in Copenhagen, Denmark, where it had been in dusty storage for nearly 50 years. The dismantled ride had been stored in 5,000 unmarked pieces, and Logan's only guide to rebuilding it was a faded picture postcard. Old German newspapers, providing backing for some of the ornate mirrors used extensively on all parts of the carrousel, authenticate its age.

Faking a German merry-go-round is well-nigh impossible because the traditional European horses always turn clockwise, while American-built merry-go-rounds turn counterclockwise. And merry-go-round horses have only one show side. Only the right-hand sides on American horses have the deeply carved manes and jeweled harnesses, which peter out quite noticeably as

---

°El Dorado was acquired in 1971 by Toshimaen Amusement Park, Tokyo, Japan. Their total investment for the ride, including a building 103 feet in diameter to house it, was $800,000. Today El Dorado accommodates 36 riders in 9 Royal Thrones on the top platform, plus 2 dozen jumping horses, 4 chariots, 6 gondolas, 4 giant tubs, and 6 funny pigs (a Japanese addition) to accommodate 118 more—a total of 154 passengers to admire the 60 paintings on the ceiling and the 1,800 lights reflected from the 4,200 gilded mirrors.

they come around from the front towards the rather plain left side. Switching the horses around, so they could be ridden in the opposite direction from the way they had been designed to go, would just about ruin their effect.

Carving horses in the great days of merry-go-round construction was a business, not an art. Because they wanted their finest carvings to be most visible, the builders did the more impressive work on the large, stationary horses on the outer rim. The smaller jumpers on the inside, which only are seen momentarily as they move up and down, have their manes on the right side and are beautifully decorated, but very few have the lavishly carved shields, flowers, armor, and fluted saddles seen on the big horses.

The craftsmen worked on a strictly commercial basis, with blockers roughing out the bodies, finishers doing the legs and heads, decorators carving the medieval trappings, and painters completing the job. All worked for the designers, many of whom became famous for their individual styles. Gustav Dentzel horses can be recognized by their perfect manes, Allen Herschell horses by their bulbous knees. Looff liked to carve dead rabbits or a brace of birds behind the saddles of his hunters, and any horse carved at the Philadelphia Toboggan Company was known for its indestructable colors.

The Philadelphia Toboggan Company built all of the largest merry-go-rounds still in existence today. One fine example of their work is the 64 footer, with 80 horses, 5 abreast, for Olympic Park, Mapleton, New Jersey. Stein & Goldstein, of Brooklyn, built the largest merry-go-rounds ever made, some holding over 100 passengers with as many as 6 horses abreast, but none are known to have survived. In the 30 years following 1904, Philadelphia Toboggan built 68 elaborate merry-go-rounds, including 4 with horses riding 5 abreast. One of the 4 was destroyed by fire in 1912 at Ocean Park in Los Angeles. Another is in Atlantic City.

A third, originally at Chicago's Riverview, spent an ignominious four years in a Galena, Illinois warehouse and wound up at 6 Flags Over Georgia in Atlanta, where it remains today. Its four 11-foot Lovers' Chariots are the most elaborately figured in the world, but they had been repainted so many times at Riverview that the staff at 6 Flags spent six months removing the thick layers

The fabulous El Dorado carousel, originally imported from Leipzig for Coney Island, is now a major attraction in Tokyo.

Even this antique merry-go-round couldn't save Freedomland. Fortunately, it has found a new home in Gaslight Village at Lake George, New York.

Detail of a merry-go-round built by Gustav Dentzel. The cost of such hand-carved work would be prohibitive today.

Looff's hunting horses often carried dead animals behind the saddle. This merry-go-round is currently at Rhode Island's Crescent Park.

of old paint to reveal the carving details. The 70 horses, also stripped down to the wood, include four battle-armored steeds from the days of King Arthur, the only four such fiery horses on any one merry-go-round and capable of going 14 mph. Their riders at Riverview included such notables as Al Capone, Tom Mix, William Randolph Hearst, President Harding, and Clara Bow.

While the big merry-go-rounds thoughtfully had chariots and gondolas for riders too young or too old to mount the horses, some of the carvers were not without a sense of humor. One of them, irked because a park owner held him to an unfavorable contract, delivered the merry-go-round horses as ordered, but deliberately embarrassed the buyer by making them leering and well-endowed stallions.

Except for Russian-born M. C. Illions, who carved circus wagons in England, and Dentzel, whose family made carrousels in Germany, the greatest American carvers all learned the trade in the United States. Large-scale manufacturing started in Brooklyn shortly after the invention of the steam engine in 1860. Before that, merry-go-rounds were limited in size and weight because they had to be turned manually, but mechanical power allowed production of rides larger than anything that could be turned by a mule, horse, sometimes the owner. By the time the traction companies began building amusement parks, manufacturing was centered in North Tonawanda, New York, near Buffalo. The little town was known as the Merry-go-round Capital of the World. At one time it was the home of three merry-go-round factories (and the birthplace of the American band organ as well).

The industry in North Tonawanda grew up around the Armitage-Herschell Company, which expanded from an engine plant, listing "steam riding galleries" as a sideline, to a shipping plant where merry-go-rounds were made at a one-per-day rate. Buyers could get an Armitage-Herschell merry-go-round for less than $2,000, and the company made so much money so quickly that local banks refused to take the company's deposits.

In the Midwest, Charles W. Parker began building merry-go-rounds in Abilene, Kansas, to cut freight costs from the East for the rapidly growing western markets. When Dwight D. Eisenhower was a teenager, he sandpapered horses at this early Parker factory. By 1911, Parker had outgrown Abilene and moved operations to a 6-story plant in Leavenworth, Kansas, where he was soon calling himself "the amusement king." Certainly, he was the world's largest manufacturer of amusement devices, getting so large that he coined his own name for his merry-go-rounds— "carry-us-alls."

In April, 1917, a historian noted after a visit to the plant that 17 carry-us-alls, 5 Ferris wheels, and 3 monkey speedways were being tested and readied for shipment at the same time. Production was overflowing plant capacity to the point where even the front yard and the building's roof were being used as work areas. Sometimes as many as 7 carry-us-alls were being worked on simultaneously on the roof.

Although the total amusement park business today is bigger than it ever was, the demand for new, big merry-go-rounds has almost died. There is demand for the big rides, but not for new ones. As traditional parks close down, their old carrousels come onto the market, destroying the demand for new 50- and 60-foot merry-go-rounds.

Though the old ones are better than today's machine-built merry-go-rounds, some of the new ones do have safer handles for kids and, sometimes, double-length saddles more like motorcycle saddles than true horse saddles, each accommodating two persons riding in tandem. George W. Long still hand carves merry-go-round horses in Rochester, New York. But his remarkably low price of $500 per horse is still a long way from the $200 or less for a cast-aluminum horse, which is also lighter in weight and therefore that much easier to pull. George Long's carving is more of a hobby than a business, anyhow, because today the cost of handcarving an entire merry-go-round is prohibitive. Nevertheless, an assembly-line horse without even a mane just doesn't compare to a merry-go-round horse carved by an artist.

A number of importers still offer European merry-go-rounds, notably Bob Meluzzi of Sarasota, Florida, who has a 48-footer sporting an authentic organ and hand-crafted wooden horses and paneling. But Kansas is still the only place left in the United States where merry-go-rounds are still being built. For example, Carl Theel, in Leavenworth, sells his 34-foot Chieftain for $12,800 in the deluxe version. It has twenty 2-abreast jumpers, 4 stationary ponies, and 2 chariots, with a 28-passenger capacity. Theel also builds specials, such as a Christmas merry-go-round with reindeer instead of horses. However, there is no way of avoiding the fact that his horses are mass-produced out of cast aluminum—and look it.

Chance Manufacturing Company in Wichita now owns the remnants of the Allan Herschell Company. The best that Chance has to offer is a 36-footer costing $36,670, which is not much different from Theel's. It has 30 jumpers—and an 8-track tape deck for a stereo system.

Actually, the best merry-go-rounds even in the great days never did have a calliope (generally pronounced kal-i-o-pee, but kally-ope to circus people). A calliope's exceedingly shrill and piercing notes can be heard at great distances when a circus pulls into town or a showboat banks at a river and is too loud for an amusement park. Thus merry-go-round music is traditionally supplied by a band organ.

In contrast to the type of organ used in dance halls and skating rinks, where the rhythm is accentuated, a carrousel organ is stronger and higher pitched with a more penetrating sound. The high registers carry the clear notes of the melody. Some band organs were as tall as 15 feet, especially those built into the double-deck merry-go-rounds, which were a fad for a while (Dentzel marketed a 2-story carrousel in 1890). Double-deckers are an example of the unsuccessful attempt at innovation in the field. They proved to be unprofitable because they were too slow to load and unload, and those around today were made in Europe. But there were other attempts at experimentation, including models with undulating platforms, with stationary platforms and wheels in each horse, with the horses facing outward (the passengers thus rode sideways, facing the bystanders), and the flying horse-type carrousel.

The flying horses aren't mounted to a platform but hang from individual rods hinged at the top so that the faster the ride turns, the more tilted the riders become. The famous old ride at Watch Hill, Rhode Island, with its flying horses swinging out as the frame turned, was first powered by hand, then by horse, eventually by water, and finally by electricity until Watch Hill's lights went out.

The flying horses evolved into many types of circular rides, starting with "captive flying machines," which are in no way merry-go-rounds. But the traditional merry-go-round is still *the* merry-go-round, the most popular ride in any park and, in one way or another, it is the direct ancestor of all of today's flat rides, including the scariest (see Chapter 6).

4: Roller Coasters

W<small>HEN</small> Aurel Vaszin got off the boat from Rumania in 1904 as a 19-year-old cabinetmaker, he didn't even know what a roller coaster was. But he has since built more roller coasters than anyone else in the world; some 45 to 50 percent of all existing American roller coasters were built by Vaszin's company, National Amusement Device Company of Dayton, Ohio.*

As Vaszin's fame spread internationally, he was commissioned to build coasters in Guatemala, Venezuela, Ecuador, Brazil, New Zealand, Iraq, England, France, Belgium, Canada, and Mexico. His $600,000 Mexico City ride is the biggest roller coaster ever built, with the first dip being an 82-foot drop, giving a sensation like falling off an 8-story building. In contrast, the biggest roller coaster in the United States is at Playland Park, San Antonio,

*As late as the 1950s, Vaszin had 75 employees in Dayton building all kinds of rides, but now he is down to less than a dozen (one of whom has been with the company almost half a century). Nowadays the little company has had a good year when two new rides are built. Vaszin got out of the amusement park business in 1935 when park patrons were so scarce that they didn't cover the cost of the 40 to 50 pounds of meat being eaten every day by the animals in the small zoo at his Forest Park.

Texas, which required 270,000 board feet of lumber for construction.

"All my rides are perfectly safe," Vaszin avers. "I have ridden them all as a matter of testing them out, and I would certainly never build anything I would be afraid to ride myself." The catch is that the peppery octogenarian isn't afraid of anything. But actually, Vaszin's genius lies in creating the illusion of danger. No Vaszin coaster exceeds 24 mph on the curves, and top speed in the valleys is 38 mph. There's a faster ride in Manchester, England, where the Bobs at Belle Vue Amusement Park has been clocked at 61 mph, but the fastest ride in the United States is the Tornado at Petticoat Junction, Panama City, Florida. Barkers try to get the public to believe that they will ride at 100 mph, but the actual speed is less than half of that. Even so, ride the Tornado and your stomach comes up to here.

On most days, gravity rides run faster in the South than in the North. On a hot day, when the packing grease is thinner, speeds will be as much as 10 percent faster than on cold days, when the grease is more viscous.

Building up suspense is an important part of the illusion of danger, and a car that does not clank ominously on its way up the initial incline is not as satisfactory as one that does. One such ride is Paragon Park's magnificent ride at Hull, Massachusetts. In addition, Paragon Park's coaster adds a turn as the cars top the crest, so that riders experience the added sensation of dropping off into space.

Height is one thrill factor, and sensations of speed are also intensified by building high-speed stretches in close proximity to other structures. Roaring under something is better yet. Conneaut Lake Park's Blue Streak is in no way a high ride, but its famous over-and-under has thrilled millions in the last half century.

The lower the car is built to the ground, the greater the sensation of speed. Likewise, the addition of railings on the runways heighten the illusion of danger as the posts flash by. Conversely, leaving the railings off the crests increases the fear of falling off.

As we said, the fear is based on illusion. Accidents on modern roller coasters are virtually unknown. Ramp ratchets, safety rails, electric block systems, and emergency brakes make them almost foolproof. Aside from Aurel Vaszin and the legendary John Allen of the Philadelphia Toboggan Company, the man who did the most to make roller coasters safe was John A. Miller, of Homewood, Illinois, who invented the antiderailment devices that keep the coaster cars locked onto the track; without them, the coaster would still be nothing but a rocky seat on wheels.

The appeal of danger makes excellent money-makers for the park operators. A determined rider could spend $20 in an hour on Coney Island's Cyclone where a ride lasted 50 seconds (40 rides an hour at 50¢ each). Capacities are as high as 3,000 passengers per hour, as on Intamin's Speed Coaster at Six Flags Over Texas.

Even with today's construction costs, a roller coaster can earn its total cost in the first season. In the 1920s, Vaszin built and operated a $39,000 roller coaster that grossed its cost in ten weeks.

Today that same ride would cost around $175,000. A small roller coaster today starts at around $65,000, not counting the cost of the land required. That's for a little coaster maybe 40 feet high with 1,400 feet of track, fabricated of 4-inch tubing. Big ones can cost up to $500,000, an investment that is feasible only in the South where the parks can be operated the year around. Northern parks have only the 90-day season between Memorial Day and Labor Day, including the rainy days when nobody shows up.

The roller coaster was born in Europe, but not in its present form. Its ancestor was the ice slide used for centuries in Russia as public amusement. At the close of the eighteenth century, a Frenchman returning from a visit to Russia decided to introduce the idea in Paris, but the warmer climate made construction of an ice slide impractical. The Frenchman's one-track mind still made him think in terms of sleds, so he built a ramp comprised of rollers, like the conveyors used on modern loading docks, down which his toboggans could slide, as if the wheel had never been invented. The Giant Slides in modern amusement parks down which kids slide sitting on pieces of carpet are directly related (the kids *walk* up to the top, too, just like the Russians).

By 1804, a roller coaster that *did* use the wheel, called the Russian Mountains, had been constructed in a public garden in the Ternes section of Paris. The news didn't travel well apparently. Well into the 1880s, amusement park operators in America were still building Artificial Sliding Hills and Artificial Coasting Courses using rollers on inclined runways.

Richard Knutsen, of Brooklyn, took out the first American patent for a roller coaster in 1878. His invention had vertical towers at each end of a double-undulating gravity track. Elevators in the towers raised the cars for the start of each new ride. The four passengers in each car sat in double-facing seats, so that two of them had to ride backward. But all that Knutsen did was get the idea; his ride was never built.

The first American coaster was finally built at Coney Island by LaMarcus Adna Thompson. Its two parallel tracks and their layout were quite similar to Knudsen's idea. Thompson's Gravity Pleasure Railway was such an instant success that he grossed as much as $500 on good days—in 1884, when a nickel really was worth 5¢.

The first roller coaster utilizing an oval design, to bring the passengers back to the starting point, the way practically all roller coasters have been built since, was the ride built less than a year after Thompson's success. Operated at Coney Island by Charles Alcoke, the 6-passenger cars were like park benches, with the passengers riding sideways so they could enjoy the scenery. Then in 1885, Phillip Hinkle built the Coney Island coaster, with a power-operated chain elevator conveying the loaded cars up the initial incline. This set the pattern for all subsequent roller coasters.

Thompson lost so much business to the two new and better rides that he decided to build the "ultimate" in roller coasters. For starters, he "adapted" the best features of both. He then invented a mechanical cable grip for the cars, which opened and closed automatically at the strategic points on the track as the cars passed over the moving power cable below them. For good measure, Thompson added dark tunnels over the first half of the ride, into which he built spooky effects alternated with pretty scenery and historical tableaus. Cars entering the tunnels tripped a switch, which flooded the scenes with electric light (still a novelty at the time)—"a surprise and a delight." Thompson built his Scenic Railway in 1887 in Atlantic City, where it immediately became so

LaMarcus A. Thompson's original Switchback Railway, the first American roller coaster, was built for Coney Island in 1884.

The largest roller coaster in the United States is at Playland Park in San Antonio.

Another relative of the roller coaster is this stainless steel slide at
Seaside Heights, New Jersey.

Coney Island's roller coaster, the Cyclone, held great appeal for thrill-seekers.

popular that he was soon building Scenic Railways for amusement parks and expositions all over the country.

World's fairs have frequently stimulated new developments in amusement devices. The Columbian Exposition in Chicago in 1893, which saw the invention of the giant Ferris wheel (see Chapter 5), also had a coaster that went all the way back to the Russian ice slides for its inspiration. The sled-cars ran down a track made of iron pipes full of freezing brine that circulated through a crude refrigerating system. Condensation created ice formations on the pipes, providing a slick surface for the coasters.

After the exposition closed, the Ice Ride was moved to Coney Island for the following summer season, and the refrigerating pipes were connected to the icebox of a neighboring saloon. In the Windy City the ride had been shaded by the great Ferris wheel, but at Coney Island it was right out under the summer sun. This caused the ice forming on the pipes to melt before it could get thick enough for the car-sleds, some of which ignominiously quit halfway down the track, leaving the disgruntled passengers to climb out and walk the rest of the way down.

Another rather silly invention was the Flip-Flap, or Loop-the-Loop, coaster. At the bottom of its gravity slope, the track was built into a complete loop. Centrifugal force prevented the riders from falling out as they went through the top of the loop upside-down. The trouble was that the car had to enter the start of the loop so fast that the rider was subjected to g-forces that were downright uncomfortable.

Riders complained of aching necks, hurting spines, and various displacements of their innards. But since this was 1888, when most people had never heard of centrifugal force and were amazed that the riders didn't fall out at the top of the loop, admission was charged at the Coney Island attraction just to watch riders foolhardy enough to try it. However, there weren't many, and none a second time, so the ride was dismantled after its second season.

Midwesterners were tougher, or perhaps just more full of beer, so the Flip-Flap Cycle Railway continued to operate at

Forest Park Highlands in St. Louis until 1906. An improved version with an elliptical loop, instead of a true circle, somewhat les-
sened the discomfort. But there was no way to turn the ride into a
money-maker, since it still was not a repeat ride. Its problems
were compounded because it could carry only four passengers in
five minutes, in contrast to a standard roller coaster carrying 24
passengers every minute, with a good percentage of them staying
on for repeats.

Modern bobsled rides utilize centrifugal force in a somewhat
more sensible manner, although a ride on one can still be quite
jolting. At the bottom of the gravity incline, the speeding cars
enter trackless runways and often bank so steeply on the sharpest
turns that they are at 70° angles. Rides such as the Wild Mouse,
where the builders deliberately ignore centrifugal force, are not
banked at all on the turns and throw their riders around unmer-
cifully. The rider who fails to get a good grip on the handrail runs
the risk of getting some bones broken on the worst of the Wild
Mouse rides. To testify to this, the grounds around some Wild
Mouse rides are strewn with everything from broken sunglasses to
false teeth lost by gasping riders as they were whipped around the
turns.

The Russian ice slides inspired still another type of coaster—
the Shoot-the-Chutes. As developed by Paul Boyton for Sea Lion
Park in Coney Island, the ride started when a loaded boat was
pulled up to the top of an elevator tower, where it was tilted
down a long, steep incline flowing with water. The boat slid down
at high speed to the receiving pool below.

Riverview's Chutes had a carefully engineered upcurve at the
bottom of the incline that shot the boats into the air before they
thumped down onto the water. The boats would then skip hard
enough across the surface to bounce the yelling passengers up out
of their seats and slam them down again. What a great ride that
was! It also incorporated a dark ride, with the boats floating
through eerie tunnels on the way to the elevator tower—great appeal for the romantically inclined.

Unfortunately, these old, wooden water rides slowly rotted to
pieces over the years, and all the great ones are gone now, and we
are left with the new flume rides, now opening in many of the

theme parks. These rides operate on the same general principle, though they are watered-down versions, as the old chutes, and, as small and as tame as they are, they often are the best rides in the park.

5: Ferris Wheels

Visitors to the 1893 Columbian Exposition in Chicago were so overwhelmed when they first saw the great Ferris wheel begin to move that they sometimes wept with emotion. The massive wheel rose to a height of 264 feet—taller than some modern 30-story skyscrapers.

Each individual car was the size of a streetcar—26 feet long and 13 feet wide, holding 60 passengers. And there were 36 of them, for a total capacity of 2,160. Riders sat in individual revolving chairs, and each loaded car weighed 15 tons.

The Ferris wheel took 20 minutes to make one majestic revolution. Rides for the privileged few (lines sometimes stretched a city block, and most exposition visitors never did get to go) consisted of two complete nonstop revolutions. The luckiest riders got on first, after the ride stopped, and spent another hour or so on the wheel as it loaded up, three cars at a time.

The Ferris wheel was so big that special engineering was necessary to allow for the expansion and contraction, caused by atmospheric changes, of its huge members. The axle, 32 inches in diameter and 45 feet long, weighed 70 tons. The weight of the two

140-foot steel towers supporting the axle was over 300 tons, and the total weight of the whole thing was nearly 3 million pounds. The cost of $380,000, or 13¢ a pound, is not bad in comparison to current prices, which are 10 to 15 times as much for most vertical rides.

The 1893 Ferris wheel, the nominal father of all amusement park Ferris wheels in existence today, was built by George Washington Gales Ferris, head of the Pittsburgh Bridge Company. When one of the speakers at a banquet given by the directors of the world's fair, a year before the opening, deplored the inability of American engineers to come up with any proposal comparable to the Eiffel Tower, Ferris was piqued. Chagrined, Ferris went home and worked up the basic idea of *the* wheel, which he based on the ideas of J. W. Graydon, a marine engineer in Washington, D.C.

After the Chicago Exposition closed, the great Ferris wheel was moved to the north side of the city, but it didn't last long as an independent attraction. When it was moved to the 1904 St. Louis World's Fair, it grossed only a little more than $250,000, barely enough to cover the transportation and erection costs. After the St. Louis Louisiana Purchase Exposition closed, the wheel was dynamited by a wrecking company and the debris sold for scrap metal.

Graydon himself designed an even bigger wheel, which was erected in London a year after Ferris built the Chicago wheel. The Graydon wheel had observation promenades at the top of each 150-foot axle tower. The hollow axle was so big that people paid to walk through it from one tower to the other. Of its 40 cars, 10 of them were elaborately furnished first class cars, with costly draperies and velvet seats, 5 were smoking cars, and the rest were for the masses. Well, it was England.

Only one other big wheel was built. In 1897, a similar big wheel was built at the Prater, Vienna's famous amusement center, and named the Riesenrad to mark the fiftieth anniversary of the coronation of Kaiser Franz Joseph. During World War II it was hit hard by American bombers, but its charred skeleton was subsequently restored, and the wheel was later featured as a setting for the movie *The Third Man*.

The big wheels have never been duplicated, although Intamin has drawn up the blueprints for a 300-foot monster. The biggest Ferris wheel in the United States today is the giant wheel now at Cedar Point. It is 148 feet tall and carries 216 passengers for a panoramic view of the Sandusky park.

The antecedents of the Ferris wheel are heavy with age. Amusement devices called pleasure wheels have been used for centuries in European and Oriental countries. In England they were called perpendicular roundabouts. They were built commercially in America as early as 1870 in Brooklyn, where Charles W. D. Dare began building a wooden 20-foot ride known as the Dare wheel. Fifteen years later in Marion, Ohio, the Strobel Manufacturing Company was building an 8-seat wooden wheel, 25 feet in diameter, rotated by a gasoline engine.

Then in the late 1880s, a change from wood to metal construction came when the Conderman Brothers of Clay City, Indiana, began building 35-foot pleasure wheels made out of metal tubing. Each of the 12 buggy-like carriages carried 2 passengers. The design was patented with 21 claims, and within a few years the Condermans were suing imitators left and right for patent infringements. These lawsuits were invariably thrown out of court because most of the Conderman patent claims were based on centuries-old principles, not modern inventions.

Eventually someone invented an even lighter Ferris wheel, one that was more mobile. After one ride in 1893 on the Chicago Ferris wheel, William E. Sullivan of Roodhouse, Illinois, said then and there, "I have discovered what I want to design and build—a portable Ferris wheel." It took him seven years to construct his first model, a 12-seat 45-footer. Then it was another six years before he was ready to start serious commercial production, partly because he had to fight off Conderman's lawsuits for patent infringements.

When Sullivan finally incorporated in 1906, he needed working capital and decided to call the new company the Eli Bridge Company to impress potential stockholders. His thinking was that an amusement device might be thought to be too frivolous, and if the day came when the fad was over, the company could always build bridges.

He needn't have worried. The Eli Bridge Company, now

under the aegis of a third-generation Sullivan, has built some 1,200 Ferris wheels. With the exception of some 30 destroyed in warehouse fires and so on, most of them remain in active operation today all over the United States, Canada, Mexico, Puerto Rico, the Philippines, Ecuador, Columbia, Chile, Argentina, Australia, New Zealand, England, and South Africa. That first 1900 Big Eli now decorates the front yard of the company's present factory in Jacksonville, Illinois, and it still works. At one time the seemingly indestructible Eli wheels were so popular that some parks operated as many as four of them simultaneously. In 1909, Eli Bridge Company built the 100-foot Seattle wheel, but the biggest park wheel they build today is the 16-car Aristocrat, 55 feet tall.

The 135-foot Wonder wheel at Coney Island was the invention of Charles Herman in 1920. Its cars, riding on built-in curved tracks within the revolving structure, rolled back and forth as the tracks inclined when the wheel was in motion. It had 16 rolling and 8 nonrolling cars, each carrying four passengers. The Dreamland wheel, an adaptation of this idea in Yokohama, has thrilled many a Japanese.

Down through the years, Ferris wheel inventors have experimented with numerous other fantastic designs. One incorporated sliding seats, which bumped violently from one spoke of the wheel to the next, but too many customers got sick to their stomachs. Another had wheels within wheels, but loading and unloading was too cumbersome a process. C. W. Parker built Ferris wheels that had small house-like cabins, instead of the more traditional buggy-type seats Eli Bridge Company made so popular. The wheel built for the 1939 world's fair in New York (now at Steel Pier, Atlantic City) had closed cages so the riders couldn't fall out.

Many modern wheels, like the Morgan Hughes Giant Ferris wheel (110-foot version), have horizontally rotating gondolas, which passengers can turn manually for a full 360° view. The Hughes 110-footer has 20 gondolas, each of which carries 6 adults, loading 5 gondolas simultaneously.

Chance Manufacturing Company makes a terrifying wheel on

which the cars can be turned radially on a rigid front-to-back axle. Called the Skydiver, the wheel's cars align with the horizon only at the top and bottom of the circle; otherwise, the car is either diving toward the ground nose first or the rider is flat on his back as the car rises toward the top. The passenger can rotate the car manually on its straight-through axle and thus ride around completely upside down if he is so inclined, or he can change the spin position of the car as he wishes. Chance gets $72,950 for the Skydiver, and with its capacity of 500 passengers per hour, it can pay for itself in a month; the Skydiver at Peony Park in Omaha has long waiting lines all season.

Chance used the same idea on a modified twin wheel, which approached a flat ride in compactness, called the Tumbler. In a portable version, the Tumbler costs $69,750, loads four 3-passenger seats at a time, and has a 720-passenger-per-hour capacity. But the Turbo is a better deal for the park than for the rider, who does not get as good a ride as offered on the Skydivers in the eastern parks.

Chance's Ferris wheel, with 16 traditional seats, carries the same price tag as the little Turbo, but it is a respectable 75 feet high and has an even better passenger capacity. Chance also builds the $135,000 double-rotor Sky Wheel, with an 8-car revolving wheel at each end of a rotating arm, as featured at California's now-defunct Pacific Ocean Park in Santa Monica. For some odd reason, the Sky Wheel is more impressive from the ground than from inside. The Rampage, which has only six cars flat against the sides of each rotating wheel, is a smaller version of the same idea, but it is scarier to ride because the swinging cars do not have footrests—the rider's legs simply hang over the edge of the seat.

Chance's Zipper is not a real Ferris wheel, but it can't be classified as anything else, either. The $56,950 ride has twelve 2-passenger cars, which turn around an ellipse that rotates itself, and the ride is 55 feet high when standing straight up. It's an Atlantic City favorite.

A double-swiveling Intamin giant wheel at Hersheypark takes the cake for fast loading and unloading. All twelve 6-passenger rotating gondolas are unloaded simultaneously on each of the two wheels. Each wheel comes down onto the ground flat, while the wheel at the other end of the massive arm rises to its apex. A model with 8-arm wheels is currently being built for Astroworld in Houston.

The Ferris wheel started out as an observation device as much as a thrill ride. A fellow could put his arm around his girl to reassure her if she got scared (or pretended to get scared) at the unusual height. But the main idea was the scenery. The observation towers and Sky Rides developed for other world's fairs are directly related to the Ferris wheel.

The Space Towers that dominate the skylines of so many amusement parks today all stem from the popularity of the 607-foot tripod Space Needle built at the Seattle World's Fair in 1962, with its revolving restaurant on top. Fred A. Picard, the Swiss cable car builder, was impressed by the long lines waiting to get to the observation tower when he visited the Seattle fair. At his San Francisco hotel, he delighted in riding up on the outside elevator, a glass cabin facing the city instead of an ordinary, inside elevator cage. Why not combine the two ideas? To think was to act with Picard, and he had a 3-foot mock-up built. On the strength of only that and his own enthusiasm, he landed a contract to erect the first Space Tower.

Various park operators refer to the 325-foot observation towers by different names. Cedar Point calls it their Space Spiral; it's the Astrotower at Coney Island and the Astroworld Spiral in Houston. Parks in Minnesota, California, Wisconsin, New Jersey, and Oklahoma have Picard's towers, too, and they have been built in many other countries as well. In Rotterdam, The Netherlands, the Space Tower is built on *top* of another 365-foot tower, and the entire 692-foot structure is called the Euromast.

The principle that helps sell so many Space Towers is quite simple—a counterweight slides up and down in the hollow core, demanding minimal power to pull the 2-story passenger cabin to the top. In the Fort Dells, Wisconsin, Space Tower passengers ride up to a height of 220 feet in a 60-passenger doughnut-like cabin that slowly rotates a full 360° as it silently rises. At the top, it rotates for two full turns. The complete ride takes less than four minutes, which means that the Dells tower has a passenger capacity of 900 per hour. A ride up the tower at Marineland of the Pacific, Palos Verdes, California, takes five minutes, which gives that park a 720-passenger-per-hour capacity and a quite respectable gross.

A related ride is being produced in Zurich by Intamin A. G., revolving "gyro" towers, although most of their observation towers built in the United States to date are custom-built jobs for theme parks. The Intamin towers are more old-fashioned than the von Roll towers, in which getting up is half the fun. For example, high-speed elevators in the hexagonal tower at Magic Mountain in California, like the similar compact 330-foot hex at the new amusement complex at Gatlinburg, Tennessee, rises to a height of 384 feet. The top half of the twin observation deck is glassed in, but the lower story is an open promenade. Intamin's tower built for Six Flags Over Texas in the shape of an oil derrick is in keeping with the theme of that park. The 330-foot observation tower in the International Street section at King's Island, Ohio, is a smaller replica of the Eiffel Tower.

The Westinghouse Air Brake Company is also making attempts to get in on the amusement business with their Space Towers, but so far they haven't met with much success. Their Sky Towers, 150 feet high, have been established at the Fun Pier in Wildwood, New Jersey, and at Ocean World, Ft. Lauderdale, Florida. But it offers little competition for the Swiss imports.

The most famous of all the towers is, of course, the 1886 Eiffel Tower, which, in turn, inspired a number of early amusement-parks observation towers. Similarly, the Eiffel Tower was inspired by the iron 300-foot Sawyer Tower at the Philadelphia Centennial Exposition in 1876, which originally had been planned as a 1,000-foot structure.* Although the Philadelphia fair commission took fright and modified the original designs, Gustave Eiffel used them in overcoming the considerable opposition to his proposal for the Paris fair.

Another precursor of the modern towers was the Bascule Bridge Company's Aeroscope observation tower built for the San

---

*When the Philadelphia Exposition closed, the Sawyer Tower was moved to Coney Island, where it came to a sad end. It was destroyed in the great Dreamland fire of 1911, when the boilers for its steam elevators blew up the whole iron structure.

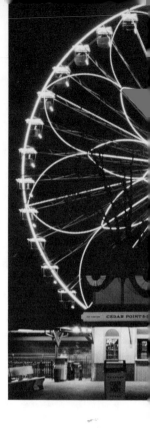

Japan's Dreamland wheel is an excellent imitation of Coney Island's famous Wonder wheel.

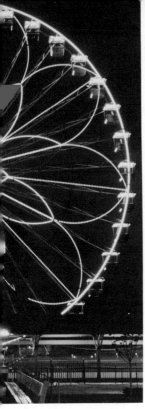

Cedar Point's giant wheel is now the largest in the United States.

An Atlantic City favorite is the Zipper, a unique adaptation of the Ferris wheel.

The 1970 Michigan State Fair featured this adaptation of the Ferris wheel, the Turbo.

(Opposite page, bottom left) Chromolithograph after the painting by Charles Graham of the original Ferris wheel at Chicago's 1893 Columbian Exposition. (Photo courtesy of the Chicago Historical Society)

Magic Mountain's Sky Ride, built by Intamin A. G., provides a thrilling alternative to the 384-foot Intamin observation tower.

The cabin of the Space Tower at Wisconsin's Fort Dells rotates a full 360° as it ascends 220 feet above the park.

Francisco Exposition in 1915. That device boasted a cage on one
end of a 240-foot swiveling arm and a 300-ton concrete counterweight on the other end. Swiveling on trunnions on a 50-foot
structure, like a large military cannon, the Aeroscope utilized an
electrically controlled water tank to equalize the weight of the
loaded cage regardless of how many passengers were in it. The
cage could lift 120 passengers to a height of 265 feet, at which
point the entire upright tower rotated on tracks at its base to give
passengers a full 360° panoramic view. A smaller Aeroscope, accommodating 50 adults in a rectangular, cage-like building at the
tip of the riser structure, was subsequently built for amusement
parks for a few years by the venerable Eli Bridge Company of
southern Illinois.

The novelty of height began to wear off with the construction
of city skyscrapers. Riverview's once heavily patronized 250-foot
steel observation tower had not been in use for many years when
it was converted to the Pair-O-Chutes ride in 1937—only to be
sold for scrap in 1967.

Another Chicago innovation, the ultimate in aerial sight-
seeing, made its appearance at the 1933 Century of Progress
World's Fair in Chicago: the Sky Ride. Its observation gondolas
crossed the lagoon, like European aerial tramways, at the
lakefront between two 190-foot towers. The modern development
of this concept stems directly from the fair, for the developer of
the aerial ride idea, Fred Picard, first had his interest piqued by
Chicago's Sky Ride. First establishing himself in winter sports
operations in Sun Valley, Idaho, he later became involved with
Paul Zuberbühler, chief engineer of the von Roll Ironworks of
Switzerland, in an effort to determine the feasibility of building
big-time ski lifts and aerial tramways in U.S. snow country.
Typically, Picard decided to combine his two passions, winter
sports and amusement parks, to determine the feasibility of the
van Roll approaches—at no risk to himself.

Walt Disney was then putting together components for his
Anaheim park, and the brash young Swiss wrangled an introduc-
tion to meet him, thereby falling into one of the best pieces of luck
anybody in his business could ask for. It seems that Disney had
only recently finished making a movie in which the cast had used

the terminal station of the Zermatt lift as a shooting location—the lift's mechanism had been built by von Roll and Disney had been fascinated. As soon as Picard heard that, he immediately launched into his sales pitch for the construction of an artificial hill with a chalet for the terminal station. Since Disney was a man of quick decision, within a matter of minutes the two were shaking hands on the deal. Picard's first Sky Ride was sold in less than half an hour.

That was in 1956. Picard has since sold dozens of Sky Rides to amusement parks all over the United States. The original von Roll Sky Ride at Disneyland celebrated the carrying of its 100-millionth passenger in 1973. With so many parks keeping an eye on Disney, his successes were imitated everywhere right from the beginning of Disneyland. Several parks ordered a second Sky Ride—not because the first one had worn out, but because there were more people who wanted to ride than one Sky Ride could handle, as at Cedar Point.

Because terrains are different, not all von Roll Sky Rides are the same, as are that manufacturer's Space Towers. The Sky Ride built for Aquarena Park, San Marcos, Texas, for example, has globular cars resembling helicopter cockpits that can be rotated horizontally by the rider for a 360° view of the ground he's passing over.

A basic von Roll Sky Ride is a mono-cable system with an endlessly moving haul rope, to which the small cars are attached by a patented cable grip. Hourly capacity is around 1,500 passengers, but von Roll builds the big stuff, too. In the summer of 1973 they finished a $1.5 million contract for the 2-mile tramway system at Gatlinburg, Tennessee. The two big cabins hold 120 passengers each, and they travel at 12 mph up a 1,400-foot mountain for some of the best sight-seeing in the entire amusement complex at Great Smoky Mountain National Park.

Intamin is in there pitching, too. The Eagle's Flight aerial tramway at Magic Mountain is an excellent way to see a good part of southern California. Suspended from 120-foot towers, the gondolas glide silently from three boarding stations, including one terminal on top of Magic Mountain itself. The bucket-type gondolas are considerably safer than the buggy-type seats or hanging chairs used by lesser competition for short-run installations, as on the piers at Atlantic City or in small parks like Glen Echo.

Compared to Space Towers, sky-lifts and Sky Rides are easy to build, and imitative competition therefore is heavier. ABM International, Dan Glosser, Halsco Engineering, Hopkins Associates, and Taylor Engineering are all bidding for their share. Goforth Brothers, Shelby, North Carolina, builds a novel Balloon Ride in which the passengers stand in a basket below a simulated hot-air balloon, similar to the one in *Around the World in Eighty Days*. Goforth's standard $52,000 Skyliner, running 28 dual chairs on 1,000 feet of endless cable, is engineered so that it can be taken down, loaded on a trailer, and moved from one location to another as a carnival ride.

The monorail, which also was a great success at the Seattle World's Fair, provided basic transportation from downtown to the 74-acre fairgrounds, as well as serving as a sight-seeing ride. Building a monorail is a major project, frequently over the heads of average park operators in more ways than one. Disney's four monorails in Anaheim cost $2.3 million, with the Alweg monorail covering a 2½-mile "highway in the sky." Magic Mountain's Metro is an *automated* monorail with a 3,700-foot running course. The monorail at Dutch Wonderland in Lancaster, Pennsylvania, carries 50 passengers; Hersheypark's 6-car monorail is probably better built than Chicago's elevated system. Even the mini-monorails, such as the one in Atlantic City at the Million Dollar Pier, are major investments, and most parks that build them do so primarily for prestige.

But if there are cheaper ways to provide for sight-seeing, few are better.

6: Flat Rides

Some 100,000 applications covering inventions for amusement park devices have been filed at the U.S. Patent Office in Washington, D.C. Many have followed developments in transportation—rides simulating bicycles, automobiles, airplanes, zeppelins, and now rockets have all been built as park flat rides.

For instance, when bicycles were still a novelty, an 1882 amusement park ride called Flying Velocipedes had bikes bolted to the outside of a circular frame, with the riders providing the power. However, too many riders shirked their share of the pedaling, and the ride was pronounced a failure.

The Whip is what most people visualize when they think of a flat ride. Its oblong platform carries as many as a dozen cars, each on a free-turning table with flexible arms attached to the moving cable, which swings them out on the turns like the snap of a whip. Ever since the whip was invented by W. F. Mangels in 1914, it has proven to be a popular thriller at parks all over the world. It is also one of the safest rides in the park, with centrifugal force keeping riders firmly in their seats as they spin around. At Dorney Park in Allentown, Pennsylvania, the Whip is right at the kiddieland entrance, where it is considered a spectator attraction.

The popular Calypso is a similar but milder device, a ride where oldsters can take the small fry without such violent spinning. The Calypso's action, although freer, can be compared to Glosser's Spinning Cups, where the 56-foot basic platform turns clockwise and the three 21-foot secondary platforms, each holding six cars turning clockwise, turn counterclockwise. With 6 passengers in each of the 18 cars, Spinning Cups has a high capacity even with a 3-minute cycle time. That's over 2,000 riders per hour.

The Rocket was one of the earliest daredevil flat rides, with its string of cars circling the track at what many considered excessive speeds. It doesn't do anything to the rider except spin him around, but it spins him around fast. The alighting rider can be so dizzy that he has trouble trying to walk in a straight line, which is good for laughs from the spectators who know better than to get on the thing. A modern version of the rocket is the Swiss Bobs, which simulates an Olympic bobsled ride. Riders on its circular, back-hill track are in full view of the spectators at all times.

At the Wisconsin Dells, there's a ride called Roc-N-Roll in which the rider cages himself for motion that would be called assault if he weren't paying for it. The entire car rotates longitudinally, like the exercise wheel in a gerbil cage, except that the Roc-N-Roll passenger is in a seat and can, if he wants to—the cars are manually controlled—somersault around the circular platform with each revolution of his cage-car.

The Dells also has one of the famous Tilt-A-Whirl rides made by Sellner. The Tilt-A-Whirl's whip-like circular track adds an undulating motion, and many people vomit when they get off it. For this reason some parks bar kids from such rides if they are thought to be too young.

The first circular, undulating flat rides—mild affairs—were built in England as far back as 1845 and were called Venetian Gondolas. An otherwise tame ride of this type, the Caterpillar, was notorious as a place to smooch as its rolling canopy came up and over the string of cars. Glosser sells a modern version called Lovers Lake, also installed in various parks with optional themes such as the Tarantella.

One of the earliest undulating flat rides was Witching Waves, built in 1907 at Luna Park in Coney Island. Its oval course had a flexible metal floor that moved up and down in wavelike motions as riders tried to steer their 2-passenger cars. Today's undulating circular rides are less demanding of passengers, who simply sit in the coasterlike cars and ride around a track with two gentle inclines. Typical rides are the Musik Express and the Matterhorn, both imported by Mickey Hughes from West Germany.

All three major importers—Hughes, Glosser, and Meluzzi—have a ride called the Himalaya, which sounds scary but is just another circular undulating ride. The Himalaya at Cedar Point is fast enough, while still being an earthbound ride, to get into the spirit of things.

Of the flat rides that lift passengers off the ground, Intamin's Drunken Barrel is one of the tamest. At King's Island, it has 18 spinning cars on a single revolving platform that oscillates up and down as it turns. The same basic ride is also made with Sombrero cars for a number of other parks.

A wilder tilting ride is the Trabant. Spin a coin on a tabletop, and as the coin slows down and its turning edges approach the surface, you have the action of a Trabant. Cars whirl around on the turning, circular platform as it rises and falls beneath them. This gyroscopic ride is even more fun at night because of the dazzling lights. Some version of the $50,000 Trabant is made by practically every flat ride manufacturer in the business. The Schwabinchen model at Cedar Point, imported by Hughes, has the cars running clockwise or European fashion. On the other hand, Frank Hrubetz of Salem, Oregon, uses tubs instead of stationary seats, and their turning adds still another dimension of motion on his $55,000 Tip Top.

Chance's Toboggan ride is somewhat of a roller coaster but is considered a flat ride because it occupies ground space of only 80 by 25 feet. The one at the Wisconsin Dells is 55 feet high. Cars are lifted to the top of a tower, around which tracks spiral down to a small series of inclines. The ride looks better than it really is—the passenger doesn't reach the speeds he thinks he will. Space alloted for the inclines at the bottom is so limited that the turns are necessarily so sharp that the jolting is uncomfortable. For the

$83,750 Chance gets for the Toboggan, a park operator could get a *real* roller coaster, if he's got the ground space.

Another amusement device, also not quite a flat ride, was the Steeplechase Race Course that was the nucleus of Steeplechase Park at Coney Island. The ride had four parallel tracks three feet high, with a roller-mounted wooden horse on each. The riders were lined up at a traditional starting gate, although there was no competition in the real racing because speed on the gravity ride was determined by the two riders' weight on each tandem-saddled horse. As the Grand National Steeplechase, it thrills riders today at Dania, Florida.

Circle swings are among the most venerable of all amusement devices. In the simplest form, seats are suspended from chains attached to a frame revolving horizontally on a central post. Many manually operated circle swings are still made for public playgrounds and school yards. The first modern circle swing was installed at Elitch's Gardens in 1904, where its carriages, hanging by cables from six radial arms, swung in sufficiently wide circles.

Competition was always keen between the parks to boast the biggest and most impressive circle swing. One was even invented by Hiram Maxim, better known as the inventor of the military machine gun. But the Maxim circle swing was so big and costly that only the largest parks—among them, Dreamland at Coney Island, Willow Grove in Pennsylvania, and Blackpool in England—could afford the investment.

Some of the most delightfully old-fashioned circle swings are the classics still being imported by Glosser, such as the ornate Chair-O-Plane. Another import has six miniature zeppelins with closed cabins mounted nose to tail on a rigid ring that rises around the mast. Another novel circle swing, Flying Elephants, has a dozen pachyderm-shaped carriages mounted on radial arms, and each elephant's motor-driven ears move up and down as the ride revolves. Glosser's top-of-the-line model is the Swing-Around, which swings riders in a 70-foot circle until they are swooshing horizontally at a 90° angle 25 feet above the ground.

A different variation of the circle swing was an airplane swing built by C. W. Parker, on which each of the five simulated airplanes hung from four chains. Geauga Lake built its own airplane swing, which was field-tested in the park manager's own front yard in 1925. Intamin tried out their Flying Dutchman—each carriage in the shape of a miniature galleon—by pressing their employees into service as testers.

The big old circle swing at Playland in Rye, New York, has been renamed the Jet ROTO, but only the name is new. Its long multi-passenger cars are still the same antiques they have always been, and the ride still is almost as much fun to take as the comparable attraction Riverview had next to the merry-go-round for so many years.

The Helicopter is a circular, off-the-ground ride in which the rider can control his height from the ground in the 2-passenger cars. The one at Peony Park, Omaha, is sometimes so full of kids that a grown-up has a hard time getting on.

The Scrambler, built by Eli Bridge, is another great old ride that's been around a lot of parks a long time. The Scrambler at Riverside Park in Agawam, Massachusetts, has highly decorated cars, each holding two riders (or three, for a cozier ride). Three radial arms hold secondary masts that in turn support four rotating cars. The sensation of speed is doubled as each counterclockwise-turning car flashes by a car swinging clockwise from the secondary mast following behind it.

A somewhat similar ride is the new Scat, made by Ventura Rides, Taylors, South Carolina, but the riders stand, not sit. A tub at the ends of the two outriggers (which turn at 8 rpm) turns at 20 rpm. The passenger begins by leaning against the side of the tub at a 30° angle, but the tub itself changes angles as the ride turns, so that the rider is almost flat on his back at one point and standing straight at another.

The Monster at Cedar Point, also, has an action similar to that of the Scrambler, but it's bigger and looks scarier from a distance because of its "hairy" arms, like the Spider built by Eyerly Aircraft in Salem, Oregon, and the Polyp imported by Hughes. The main distinction between these rides is that the radial arms of the Spider are menacingly curved, like a tarantula ready to come toward you. Predecessor of the Spider was Eyerly's frequently imitated Octopus, the first ride where passengers rode in spinning cars at the end of rising and falling arms as the entire device revolved. The Octopus, the first thing you see when you enter Peony Park, sets the mood for your entire visit.

Hrubetz's $40,000 Paratrooper ride is another outstandingly successful amusement device. Even when the parks are closed and the ride stands idle, it still looks more dangerous than it is. The seats swing freely below their parasols, which are also hinged on the rotating carrying frame. Kids at Peony Park do not elbow the grown-ups off this one. On the other hand, the $62,000 Hrubetz Hurricane deserves to be more popular than it has been to date. Hurricane passengers ride in six 4-passenger cars, suspended from radial arms mounted to the top of a 35-foot pylon. The cars climb to a horizontal level, from which they zoom down, climb, and zoom again.

Circular rides in which the radial arms are center-mounted to a sleeve that rises up the mast are increasing in popularity. They provide an added dimension of motion for the articulated arm action. The circular ride at Disneyland, built by Intamin in the shape of a vertical spaceship, for example, has cars that simulate rocket jets. The circling rockets pick up an amazing amount of speed as they dip and zoom with individual manual controls.

Eyerly's Loop-O-Plane—built as the Mallet by imitators—has a fixed passenger car at the end of a counterweighted, vertical arm. As the car swings back and forth like a pendulum, it goes higher and higher until it performs a full loop all the way around after a couple of agonizing, almost full swings, including one when the car is upside down at the top of the swing and hangs momentarily before inching its way to complete the 360° arc. Attendants at Riverview sometimes made extra money by picking up the change that fell out of the Loop-O-Plane riders' pockets. Mallets most usually are mounted in pairs, with the parallel car arms swinging in opposite directions to equalize stresses on the mast and to give riders the impression that they are going twice as fast as they really are each time the cars swing past each other.

Eyerly also builds a similar Roll-O-Plane, in which a center-pinioned vertical arm has a car at each end that the rider can control for radial turning. The Roll-O-Plane does not rock back and forth but turns just in one direction for an effect like a 2-car Skydiver.

The ultimate variation of the Loop-O-Plane is the Super

Loop, a vertical 360° circle of track in which a whole train of cars pendulums back and forth until it builds enough momentum to complete the full circle. It is a dangerous ride, and the passengers really do have to hang on to keep from falling out.

Another ride that depends on gravity to make it scary is the Hrubetz Roundup, a $52,000 park ride adapted from an old fun house idea. Riders stand against the inner walls of a 48-foot tub. As it revolves, centrifugal force presses them against the walls with enough force so the spinning tub can be tilted to an almost vertical degree. At Geauga Lake in Aurora, Ohio, the rider is as high as the passing monorail when the tilted Roundup is at its apex. Chance makes a comparable $80,000 ride called the Rotor, which does not tilt, but rather the floor of the spinning tub is lowered away from the riders' feet as it builds up enough speed to generate the necessary centrifugal force.

The first new type of ride to come along in a long time is the recently developed Pillow Ride. G&S Amusements, Fountain Valley, California, call theirs the Jumping Jack ride. Bob Regehr, Hutchinson, Kansas, calls his version the Moon Walk, because when the patron walks across the inflated floor he does indeed look like he is walking on the low-gravity surface of the moon.

A Pillow Ride is not really a ride; the customers just amuse themselves by jumping up and down. Pillow Rides are tremendous money-makers for the parks because their initial costs are so low. They sell for as little as $1,350 for an enclosed unit 14 feet in diameter, including a repair kit (they spring leaks, so stay off if you are wearing golf shoes). Busy parks have recovered their entire investments on a single weekend with even big 32-foot Pillow Rides.

The Dodgem is another flat ride where the rider largely amuses himself, although he is riding in a car. He is completely free to steer his electric car anywhere he likes in the Dodgem hall, and the fun is in seeing how hard he can bump into somebody else who tries to dodge him. Power is provided through a pole from each car reaching up to contact the electrically charged ceiling. It is based on the same principle used by electric trolleys.

Getting patrons off at the end of a ride period is simple—the attendant simply shuts off the electricity.

The modern Dodgem dates back to 1923, when various inventors who had been suing each other for decades got together to form the Dodgem Corporation. But it was still many years before all litigation was settled, notably because Lusse Brothers were building a ride in Philadelphia called the Scooter, which was still so like the Dodgem that even many park operators use the names interchangeably. Starting out with open carriages, both makes eventually evolved as miniature automobile rides and grew to be so popular that the Dodgem (Scooter) building was often the largest structure in the park. Today the world's biggest Scooter operation is at Playland, Rye, New York.

With more than 75 years of experience, Lusse now dominates the business, although some of the best bumper cars are being made in Montreal by North American Rides. The tough, little fiberglass cars are not inexpensive—about $1,000 apiece. Italy, too, contributes to the Dodgem craze. A big part of Meluzzi's business is the construction of elaborate Scooter buildings, and one of his Italian rides is an electric speedway featuring 16 Ferrari-designed cars, with 5-speed shifts, capable of doing 45 mph.

Dark rides have an even older heritage than the Dodgem. Some of their old hand-carved wooden cars are museum pieces. The cars, passing through dark tunnels, have carried many millions of people deliciously scared by mechanical ghosts, huge plastic spiders whose eyes light up red, menacing papier-mâché pirates, and hungry-looking dinasours which pop up alarmingly.

Many of the dark rides are imported from Europe, notably Pinfari's double-deck House of Horror and triple-deck Witch's Mill. Leading U.S. builders of dark rides include the imaginative Funni-Frite Industries of Columbus, Ohio, the over-priced Mesmore & Damon of New York City, the ho-hum Pretzel Amusement Ride Company of Bridgeton, New Jersey, and Danforth Brothers with their new Flight Thru Space ride. The vehicles in many dark rides are boats rather than cars, originating with the much-imitated Old Mill built in 1902 by George Schofield in New York.

Boat rides in the open are popular at every amusement park that has waterways. New York's Prospect Park had an Aquatic Carrousel as early as 1878, a circular pontoon powered by undependable sails. Riverview's improvement of the same general idea featured motorized swans. Opryland's log raft ride was built by Switzerland's Intamin, which also builds conventional towboat rides, circular hydro saucers for independent operation, and the sight-seeing boats with electric outboard motors used at Six Flags Over Mid-America near St. Louis.

Larger boats, built specifically for amusement parks, often simulate riverboats of the Civil War era, such as the $46,000 36-foot catamaran *Daisy Belle* built by North American Rides. Cedar Point's delightful *Catawba* has a paddlewheel at the stern, plus dual crown-tipped smokestacks flanking the upper-deck pilothouse. Cruising around the park's inner island, the *Catawba* provides one of the best ground-level sight-seeing rides in the Midwest.

Cedar Point also has some excellent miniature railroads used for sight-seeing. The first miniature railroads were used at the Philadelphia Centennial Exposition in 1876, which had 14 of them in operation. They became so popular that one builder, T. G. Cagney of East Orange, New Jersey, built 1,200 of them after one of his models won a gold medal at the 1904 World's Fair in St. Louis.

Miniature railroads are not usually thought of as flat rides because they are closely related to the monorails. There are, however, many miniature railroads smaller than the Dodgem building in many parks; thus this is the reason for classifying them as a flat ride. Almost any self-respecting amusement park has always had one. Some parks, such as Cedar Point, have as many as four trains in operation simultaneously.

Like the merry-go-round, the miniature railroad *is* fit for little kids. In fact, it is often the first amusement park ride a toddler gets to enjoy. To a bug-eyed two-year-old, a ride behind the chugging engine, with its tooting whistle, is as thrilling as a ride on the Cyclone is for a teenager. But the miniature steam railroad is in no way solely a kiddie ride. *Everybody* rides the miniature railroad, including Grandma. Some 60 percent of all riders are adults.

However, it is unfortunate that a great many miniature railroad engines are the worst kind of fakes. These often consist of a slapdash, fiberglass or tin body, simulating that of a real locomotive (usually diesel) and a gasoline engine. The fake is often found in kiddielands because diesel engines are the only kind of real locomotives the kids have ever seen. Steam-powered miniature railroad engines, however, evoke an important part of Americana. Some early trains, as at Hersheypark before World War I, made no attempt at simulating a real railroad train at all. The park figured that the scenic ride itself was enough of an inducement to ride. The best miniature railroads today, however, have many of the details of the big old-timers.

The best miniature railroads powered by real steam are built by Crown Metal Products, Wyano, Pennsylvania. All Crown locomotives are of the American type 4-4-0 wheel arrangement, which was standard on U.S. railroads for over 100 years.

Like the actual railroads, miniature railroads are classified by the distance between the rails on the track. Crown's 15-inch Little Toot usually runs on a 1,250-foot track for a running time of three minutes. Station time is another three minutes. Although all the seats load and unload simultaneously at a depot long enough to accomodate all cars, many of the riders are too young or too old to move in and out very fast. But at 10 rides per hour, a 5-car 15-gauge has an hourly capacity of 500 riders, which makes the little $10,000 locomotive a very good investment indeed for the park operator.

Crown's 24-gauge locomotive has a cab the engineer looks out of instead of over, during the 5-minute ride. Track for this size engine ($17,318, F.O.B. Wyano) is usually twice as long as for a 15-gauge layout. In Arlington, Six Flags Over Texas paid Crown $77,500 for one of its 36-gauge locomotives, which pulls 480 people in six cars on a 1-mile ride. The ride takes 12 minutes, including the 3-minute depot time nobody seems able to beat.

Then there is American Keystone Associates in Irwin, Pennsylvania, which rebuilds *real* steam locomotives for park use. The 36-gauge engine, now operating at Opryland in Nashville, was originally built for hauling cotton and sugar cane for the well-known Enterprise Plantation in Patoutville, Louisiana. The antique locomotive on the Lahaina-Kaanapali & Pacific Railroad in Hawaii is a similarly restored, full-size, meant-for-business engine. American Keystone is operated as a labor of love by a couple of dedicated railroad buffs, Carl Auel and A. E. LaSalle, who also maintain an operating railroad museum in Hilliard, Florida, the Trains of Yesterday Museum.

Other parks operate scaled-down replicas, such as the three-fourths scale replicas of the famous Texas and General steam locomotives, running at Six Flags Over Georgia. And Harold Chance, who always has something to offer, has a scaled-down model of the famous 1863 4-2-4 C. P. Huntington, a near-exact one-third size replica. Unfortunately it is powered by a 4-cylinder Ford gasoline engine complete with automatic transmission. Chance gets up to $52,700 for his 10-coach package in 24-gauge, but it pulls 140 passengers per trip.

Aurel Vaszin's National Amusement Device Company has built a lot of miniature railroads, too. Starting in the early 1960s, the company installed dozens within the next few years. The $60,000 layout at LeSourdsville Lake has a reproduction of the Union Pacific's old 58, providing a very nostalgic ride indeed. National is also known as a leading producer of the related trackless trains that operate on the promenades of so many amusement parks, mostly for the benefit of people whose feet hurt.

The only rides that have ever competed seriously with miniature railroads are the miniature automobile rides of today. Scores of major parks have set aside running courses for the self-powered super-compacts. Many midget autos are built as gasoline engine sports cars, but many more are replicas of antique cars, often built on the chassis of an electric golf cart. The biggest American builder is Arrow in California, with the biggest importers being Hughes, Glosser, and Meluzzi.

A few whiz, but most chug. No driver's license required.

Do-it-yourself amusement on the individually controlled Dodgem.

Among the tamer versions of the Whip is the Calypso.

Eli Bridge's Scrambler has been a thrilling attraction at amusement parks for many years.

Centrifugal force prevents riders
from falling as the Roundup tilts.

This Super Loop in Tampa, Florida,
turns its passengers upside down.

The Rocket is one of the earliest daredevil flat rides.

The Trabant is perhaps the most popular modern circular ride.

Hersheypark's helicopter ride is a modern adaptation of the circle swing.

The Grand National Steeplechase in Dania, Florida, was once the nucleus of Steeplechase Park at Coney Island.

No park would be complete without its miniature railroad like the one at Dogpatch, U.S.A.

Rides like this boat tank have lost popularity with today's sophisticated youngsters.

Animated characters like these pirates at Disneyland have thrilled many a dark ride patron. (Photo © 1967, Walt Disney Productions)

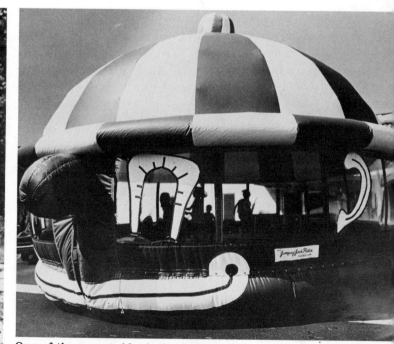

One of the newest rides is the Jumping Jack, manufactured by G & S Amusements, Fountain Valley, California.

Part 3

THE CONCESSIONS

7: The Games

"No American amusement park which permits and fosters games of chance can escape public scorn," William F. Mangels once said. But, then, Mangels was a ride man. Games are a ride man's competition because seven out of ten spenders on the midway at almost any traditional park spend more money on games than they spend on rides.

As for games of chance, the key word is *chance*. From the beginning the patron has very little chance of beating the odds on amusement park games, and when the operator isn't satisfied with the odds, he "gaffs" his wheel besides. Then the patron has *no* chance. Right? So Mangels's disdain is partially justified.

But what would the midways be without the clattering Wheel of Fortune? This game of chance is often known as a Plush Wheel today because the prizes are most frequently plush animals. But whatever it's called, what the game actually amounts to is vertical roulette—though sometimes the odds on a Wheel of Fortune can be three times as tough as on the roulette wheels in Las Vegas.

Today's gambling games, especially the crooked ones, are called flat games. This term is a holdover from the days when the

Wheel of Fortune was run horizontally, exactly like a Monte Carlo roulette wheel, and, indeed, the word "flat" in any context, except in reference to flat rides, is an anathema to most park operators today. The stuffed shirts among park operators would also like to get rid of the term hanky-pank because of its connotations. But hanky-pank is the only universally recognized term that exists in the trade to designate midway activities.

From the Mouse Run to the Milk Bottle Pitch, all games are hanky-panks, and all are operated under the control of the quay boss, whether or not he prefers to be called a games supervisor. The quay boss runs the show, and very few quay bosses today will alow games on the lot where the patrons gamble for money. Today's games of chance involve only prizes—preferably big enough to be seen by all as the winners carry them around the park as a form of free advertising. The quay boss also is on the look-out for fraud. Gaffing a wheel (just putting tension on a string around the axle, attached to a foot pedal, will do the trick), for example, is frowned upon—though not unknown—since an experienced operator can stop the wheel at will on any number.

Generally, in fact, the midway is fairly clean these days, partly because of quay boss control. Fraud is bad public relations. Indeed today, partially because it was once a money game, it's hard to find even a Mouse Run on the midway.

In this game, a live mouse is put in the center of a table and a bowl is placed upside down over him. The rim of the table has holes around its perimeter into any one of which the mouse can run when the bowl is lifted. Each patron selects a numbered hole; whoever picked the hole into which the mouse runs wins the prize.

The Mouse Run is extremely easy to gaff. If the operator surreptitiously touches a little vinegar to the edges of the hole he wants the mouse to run into a minute or so before the bowl is lifted, the mouse will head for that particular hole almost every time—provided it is a male mouse.

Another reason the Mouse Run is seldom seen anymore is because the game is difficult to run. Sometimes the mouse becomes so blasé that he's asleep when the bowl is raised. Or sometimes weisenheimers in the crowd threw corn into the table enclosure, and the mouse would sit there and eat the tidbits instead of properly running into a hole. Local chapters of the SPCA made trouble for Mouse Run operators, too. Although admittedly the amusement park mouse led a better life than his wild cousin destined to be eaten alive by some cat.

A game of chance more ordinarily seen today is the Birthday Joint, most often operated with a large 14-sided roll block. Each of 12 sides is printed with the name of a month; the other two are house sides, giving the house 6 to 1 odds that nobody will win, even when *all* 12 months are covered at the counter. Crazy Ball, a similar hanky-pank, has grown to be so popular that it has been adapted as a dart game called Crazy Darts with the same scoring system. Variations use blocks all the way from 20-sided color blocks down to 6-sided blocks, which work similarly to regulation dice.

About the only widely played games using real dice are the Horse Race games, with each player's marker proceeding around the track according to how many pips come up at his cast of the dice. The use of weighted and shaved dice is not unknown in gaffing this game, which makes a travesty of the Chuck-a-Luck cage.

Contrary to widely held opinion, the primary purpose of gaffing amusement park games is not just to cheat the customer but also to allow a shill to win. Nobody is going to play a game very long if the house does all the winning, and an operator apparently losing his shirt will attract large crowds pressing to get in on the action. The "winner" periodically takes his prizes around to the back of the booth and changes hats to come back and win some more. Most hat men working today are clean-cut college students on their summer vacations, and they usually work as roving ambassadors for a number of games in the park.

Another gambling concession is the raffle. Most traditional amusement parks generate a great deal of volume by hosting industrial picnics, fraternal outings, and similarly organized affairs. A highlight at hundreds of such outings is the announcement of the raffle winners, for which lottery tickets have been sold for weeks in advance. Gambling, pure and simple—and all with the sanction of the community. Is it any wonder that amusement parks most often disagree with Mr. Mangels's pronouncement?

If Bingo games are okay for churches to operate, what's so heinous about the Bingo Parlor at an amusement park? Some parks call the same game Lotto or even Keno (a mean gambling game in Nevada). True, the really big prizes displayed on the top shelf have to get dusted once in a while to allay the suspicious and even replaced after glittering up there so long that they are out of date. But of all Count-and-Peek stores, the Bingo game is the most difficult to gaff. The prizes given out are often the cheapest kind, but there *are* legitimate winners at every game.

Even the most blue-nosed antigamblers seldom object to the String Game, although there is absolutely no element of skill involved in playing it. Hundreds of prizes are displayed, from lowly key chains and plastic combs on the bottom shelf to electric toasters and wristwatches on the top shelf, where they can be seen from afar. A string attached to each prize passes through a hanger on the ceiling, and the ends of all the strings dangle in front of the patron. He is simply invited to pull a string to see what prize is attached to the other end. Strings on the big prizes, which may end a bit above where the patron can reach them, are changed from time to time as they discolor with age.

Even the lowly Fish Tank, smiled upon indulgently by all, is a game of chance. As the patron triumphantly hooks his fish (or more likely today, a dry roly-poly duck or clown), he most often finds a number 1 on the bottom of it, which entitles him to any prize he likes—on the first shelf. Of all the Everytime hanky-panks, the Fish Tank is second only to the Grab Bag in attracting the youngest gamblers in the park.

Many grown-ups prefer a game of skill, such as throwing baseballs at something they can knock over for a prize. The Milk Bottle Pitch has never been surpassed in popularity. Its three cast aluminum milk bottles (they used to be made of iron), set up in the form of a pyramid with the bottom of the top one resting on the other two below it, have to be knocked off their platform with three baseball pitches. Sounds easy? After the 3-unit pyramid has been knocked down and there is perhaps only the bottom of one remaining bottle facing the ball thrower, it presents a very small target indeed, and *all* three bottles have to be knocked *off* the platform before a prize is won. Operators who use eccentrically weighted baseballs or magnetized platforms are practically unheard of these days; they are not necessary.

Another easy-looking favorite using baseballs is the Cat Pitch, where the patron can win a prize in three pitches merely by tipping over three of the dozens of fluffy animals standing shoulder to shoulder at the back of the store. Simple? The solid bodies on those cats comprise less than a third of their total apparent width, most of which is light fluff standing straight out from the sides. A hurled baseball can pass through that airy fluff without so much as disturbing the cat's whiskers.

The always popular Dish Rack is another fooler. A lattice made of 4-inch boards four inches apart, in both vertical and horizontal directions, presents a surface of 4-inch openings. There's a piece of breakable china behind each opening, and it seems as if anybody throwing a ball at the framework has a 50-50 chance of hitting one of the dishes because they are only four inches apart. But the mathematical odds are not 1 to 1 but rather 3 to 1 in any given 64-inch area 48 square inches of which is board surface. Furthermore, unless the ball goes through the opening cleanly, it won't break the dish, which makes the actual target area very small indeed.

In the interests of security, many parks prefer tossing games to the more violent hurling games. Over the years, the Cane Rack has become a permanent fixture at many parks, and one of the best-known cries on the midway is, "The cane you ring is the cane you win!" Most parks buy tossing rings that vary from 1⅛"–1¾" in diameter, depending on how many canes they want to be carried around the park. If the Cane Rack is near the entrance, the patron walks away with a swagger cane more often than not. Standard 33-inch bamboo canes cost the park only 6¢ apiece, and even sparkle-headed batons with silk cords and tassels are only about 20¢ in gross lots.

The Coke Bottle Rack is another money earner. A solid rack of Coke bottles, all shoulder to shoulder, has so many bottle-neck targets that it seems impossible not to ring one. Not so. The rings have to land at the correct horizontal angle as well as at the right spot actually to ring the neck of a bottle.

Throwing hoops at a block pitch is
trickier than it looks.

The old Wheel of Fortune h
become the Plush Wheel at Linco
Park, North Dartmout
Massachusetts.

The innocuous looking String Game is still just another game of chance. (Photo courtesy of Irving Fitzig)

This easy looking Cat Pitch at Revere Beach, Massachusetts, has mostly air to throw at.

The hoops tossed in a Block Store range in size from 3¾" to 7" in diameter, depending on whether the game is a Cigarette Block, Statue Block, or whatever. In all cases, merely ringing the prize does not make a winner; the hoop must settle flat to the table around the block on which the prize stands. The operator will show doubters that the hoop will indeed fit around the block under the binoculars on the top shelf, even if he has to press the hoop into a elipse when the binocular block is slightly rectangular.

A Block Store is usually a center joint; that is, it is not along the sides of the midway but rather out in the middle so patrons can throw hoops from all four sides of the booth. The reason is because the shelves in a typical Block Store are set up like a tiered pyramid; as hoops bounce off missed targets on an upper shelf, they fall to the lower and wider shelves, where lesser prizes rest on smaller-sized blocks. The lower blocks are quite easy to ring, especially accidently. The average Block Store is a type of Everytime called a Tilyou—you pitch 'til you win. Legend has it that George C. Tilyou, the owner and operator of Steeplechase Park in Coney Island, got his name from this early type of enterprise.

Another variation of the toss game uses coins rather than rings. The Electric Pitch involves a flat board, almost completely covered with electric contact points, at which the patron tosses a coin in the hopes of touching two or more contacts as it comes to rest to complete an electric circuit. An even more common coin-tossing game is the Glass Pitch, where the patron tosses a coin at a shallow dish in the hopes that it will stay in the dish (no, Virginia, flipping the coin through the air will only make it bounce *out* of the dish instead of sliding off the back edge).

A related hanky-pank is the Basket Joint, where the patron attempts to toss a softball into what looks like an ordinary peach basket, in the hopes that the baseball will stay inside of it. The special 5-ounce ball bounces out of the taut bottom of the commercially sold Marshal Baskets for all but those who toss the ball in a low arc at the side of the tilted basket.

Shooting galleries have always been popular, particularly cork galleries, where cork gun-wielding patrons can shoot down celluloid dolls they can claim as prizes. So have Ping-Pong Rifles, shooting at cards. Even suction-cup archery.

One of the most heavily patronized gallery games anywhere is Feltman's Mow-'Em-Down machine-run gallery. In one version for hanky-panks, the patron gets 100 shots at a paper target for 50¢ with an authentic-looking, air operated tommy gun. If he can shoot out the star on the target (*completely* out, including all points of the star), he wins a prize. This is not easy with BB ammunition. Feltman supplies paper targets with either a 1″ or a 1¼″ star.

Balloon Darts is another hanky-pank that is a lot of fun even if the prizes seldom amount to much. Popping an inflated balloon by throwing darts at it is satisfying enough for most customers because they think of balloons in terms of the 25¢ to 50¢ they pay to the Balloon Man, instead of in terms of the 65¢ per gross the dart balloons cost.

Then there is the Hi-Striker, which is in a class by itself. This is where the patron takes off his coat, rolls up his sleeves, and whams a mallet at a low board to catapult a weight to the top of a high column and ring a bell. The operator can keep the carrying wire so slack that even Paul Bunyan couldn't ring the bell, but these days the parks *want* all the show-offs to look good for their girl friends, so there are more winners than not. If the prize on a 25¢ Hi-Striker is a 6¢ Pirate Flag (wholesale), everybody's happy.

Today's Guess-Your-Weight (or -Age) hanky-pank works on the same basis as the Hi-Striker, only more so, because the operator himself controls the prize-winning. Some parks hire downy-cheeked high school boys to run the Weight Scale, who are instructed to apologize that "It's my first day on the job" all summer long, as they hand out prizes to one and all. A great deal of "slum,"—prizes—including two-tone police whistles, necklaces, expansion bracelets, flutes, water pistols, and even small penknives, costs only a penny or two per prize when bought in volume. The operator willing to spend a nickel per prize can hand out a yo-yo, 12-inch giant comb, gyroscope, checkers set, 4-inch chenille animal, harmonica, or full set of playing cards.

Other hanky-panks also include Shear Joints, where artists

cut out the patron's silhouette from a piece of paper; Mitt Camps and other fortune-telling stores; jewelry engravers; T-shirt stencilers; and similar gypsy operations.

And lastly among the games is the Bozo joint. Television's Bozo the Clown may not even know it, but he got his name from the hanky-pank Bozo who sat perched on a board over a tub of water, hurling insults at patrons who were throwing baseballs at a target that they hoped would trigger the board and dump him into the water. A Bozo good at his job could so enrage customers that they would start throwing the baseballs directly at him, instead of at the 6-inch target, and for that reason the amusement park Bozo now always sits behind a protective screen.

In its heyday, Riverview had 50 different hanky-panks and called itself The World's Greatest Amusement Park. That was actually small potatoes, though, when some of the parks farther east are considered. Tony's Amusement Park, only 150 air miles east of Chicago in Bay City, Michigan, has 80 games today. Sea View Playland in Dennisport, Massachusetts, has 85, and Ocean City's Playland in New Jersey has 100. The Central Pier in Atlantic City has twice that many; Crystal Beach in Elizabethtown, North Carolina, also has 200 games. The current record is the full 285 games at Holidayland in Oceanside, California, halfway between Los Angeles and San Diego.

All of them pale in comparison to the array of games at Takarazuka Familyland in Hyogo, Japan: 690. What a place for a hat man!

8:   The Refreshments

Nothing is very refreshing about a lukewarm frankfurter laid out in a crumbly bun with maybe a glop of watery mustard smeared across it. But amusement parks are not complete without refreshment stands. Most refreshments dispensed at amusement parks are sold at grab joints, where the customer is expected to walk away with what he buys. The food is not supposed to be nourishing, healthful, or even good tasting—just fun.

And a good half the fun at Nathan's in Coney Island was getting *to* the counter, where the crowds were always at least as important as today's monosodium glutamate in making each bite a delight. Nathan's was the best grab joint Coney Island ever had.

Irresistible smells, brilliant lights, and nickel-plated rotisseries flashing as they turn, all draw millions to the grab joints at every major amusement park in America. The finest meal at a typical grab joint consists of a hot dog, a frosted root beer, and a donut. Nothing is served that takes long to prepare. For example, grab joints serve soft drinks in bottles, but they don't make ice cream sodas. A good counterman can deal 300 hot dogs per hour.

A Coney Island is a common name for a hot dog, having been

Nathan's probably has always been the best grab joint at Coney Island.

Ranking second only to hot dogs in volume of sales, popcorn seems to taste best when served hot and well buttered out of a popcorn wagon.

The messiness of ice-cream cones only adds to the fun. (Photo courtesy of Bill Mitchell)

irvented there in the 1870s. Ironically, the best Coney Islands in the world are sold not at Coney Island but rather by pushcart vendors around the perimeter of Central Park in Manhattan—with sauerkraut.

During the 1930s, Chicago's Riverview Park featured hot dogs with the sausage actually measuring 12 inches long. That's why all hot dogs have been called foot-longs in most amusement parks ever since. The foot-long of today seldom measures more than five or six inches in length, of course, but few concessionaires refer to it by any other name—certainly never as a frankfurter.°

Popcorn sales rank second only to hot dogs as amusement park refreshments. A replica of an old popcorn wagon can cost $10,000 or $15,000 these days, so it's understandable why 2¢ worth of raw corn costs the patron 25¢ after it's popped. It's worth it, especially when the vendor serves the popcorn in a paper bag; if he knows what he's doing, he pours melted butter on the interior sides of the bag, so that the customer can see that he is getting a lot of butter. Generously salted, it's just great! And it subsequently sells a lot of root beer, too. One of the best popcorn wagons in America is at Bay Beach Amusement Park in Green Bay, Wisconsin. In fact, they *guarantee* that you will get your fingers greasy.

Few people can go to an amusement park without buying cotton candy for everybody in the family. The vendor makes ten 25¢ cones of cotton candy out of one pound of ordinary sugar, but so what? Eating this fluffy stuff is like eating air, but it is fun. Colored pink at the better parks, it always tastes good—best when eaten to the sound of merry-go-round music.

Hot roasted peanuts in the shell have an appeal all their own. The taste is unimportant; the appeal is in casually throwing the empty shells over your shoulder as you walk through the park. Really *hot* roasted peanuts do indeed taste good, but they are

---

°The name "hot dog" evolved in a unique way. The small German sausages were sold by vendors who cried, "They're red hot! Get your red hot dachshund sausages!" One day in 1900 Tad Dorgan, the New York newspaperman, heard this cry and wanted to mention it in his column, but he couldn't spell "dachshund." The result: hot dog.

found only in the traditional parks. The new theme parks are so uptight about cleanliness that most of them won't even sell chewing gum, lest the customers drop the unsightly wrappers onto the ground. That's why most modern parks feature things like ice cream cones or ice cream sandwiches, where the customer eats everything he buys, including the container.

Ice cream cones are schlobber refreshments—the more messed-up the customers get, the more they enjoy the delight. The kid plastered with ice cream from chin to eyebrows has the best time of all. An ice cream cone is so important a part of the visit to an amusement park that two kids short in the money department go divvies, pooling their limited funds to buy a single cone both can enjoy a lick at a time.

Cracker Jack, the original caramel corn plus candied peanuts in the heavily waxed carton, is never given to two children to share—there's invariably too much fighting about who gets the prize. Sadly, the prizes have deteriorated in value proportionately as the prices have gone up. The once-great prizes—magic tricks and ventriloquists' whistles—have now been replaced with plastic gewgaws often not even worth taking home.

Italian Ice ("slush" in the trade)—flavoring syrup poured over a paper cup of shaved ice—is seen mostly in the East. Too bad. Frozen chocolate-covered bananas, popsicles, and even taffy apples all leave refuse frowned upon by most modern park operators. The most favored confection is the eat-it-all-up frozen custard serving, a high-profit margin soft ice cream that people have been brainwashed into eating at the Dairy Queen and similar roadside establishments.

But what the amusement parks need are more concessions like the ones at Atlantic City selling homemade candy and saltwater taffy. You can't get stuff like that anywhere else in the world.

As usual, no other amusement park even comes close to Tokyo's Toshimaen Park in its total number of refreshment stands —70 of them. Cedar Point has almost half that many, however, and Magic Mountain north of Los Angeles (which claims that it's a theme park but isn't) has 32. Rockaway's Playland manages to pack in six grab joints, even though the entire park is only the size of a city lot. The other New York Playland, at Rye, has 23.

Size aside, quality also varies. Nashville's Opryland is second to none in serving horrible food. But who can resist a Jam Session (hot dog with chili slopped on it)? Or a Bayou Cache (open-faced tuna sandwich on a sesame seed roll)? Opryland, in fact, has a lot of sit-down cafes, serving an amazing variety of fried food—food of a quality that will give the Michelin-starred restaurants no competition. Opryland patrons not attracted to Tenn-Tucky Ham-What-Am sandwiches or Belgian waffles can go to the Country Kitchen for a before-the-war breakfast or to the Casa Bonita for a Brimstone Bowl (chili, Texas style). The simulated New Orleans Coffee Mart serves a Cajun's Choice—hot corned beef on rye—which Nathan's would be ashamed to allow on the counter.

Sit-down restaurants are not really a part of a "real" amusement park image in the first place, even though some parks have many. Disneyland, of course, has 12 full-fledged restaurants, and Cedar Point outdoes the Anaheim operation with 13 chair joints. Neither matches the Tivoli in Copenhagen, with 20.

For its food and service, the best restaurant in an amusement park in the United States is at Dorney Park in Allentown, Pennsylvania. Their Pennsylvania Dutch cooking is done by people who like Pennsylvania Dutch cooking, complete with seven sweets and seven sours at each meal.

Dorney Park also has a cafeteria, as do many other amusement parks, particularly those around the Catskill area of New York. Park City in Utah even has two cafeterias, as does Mile-High Park in Denver. Ocean Beach, New London, Connecticut, has a couple of cocktail lounges, something of a rarity in the amusement park business, where anything stronger than beer is seldom for sale. Old-time ice cream parlors, such as the excellent one at Frontier City, Oklahoma City, are another rarity. In short, the average amusement park patron does not like to sit down to eat; he prefers to nibble as he strolls. If he does want to sit down to a decent dinner, he goes to a steak house downtown, not to an amusement park.

Picnic fare is something entirely different. Here the food does taste good, because Ma brought it from home. Fraternal and company picnics sometimes feature an ox roast, in which an entire side of beef is barbecued on a spit. But the staples at most picnics are still cold fried chicken, potato salad, hard-boiled eggs, and baked beans, with all the little kids burning their fingers as they try to toast marshmallows. How come a marshmallow that has been utterly ruined by accidentally catching on fire tastes so good?

Smoked eels at Stricker's Grove in Cincinnati, baked clams at Old Orchard Beach in Maine, ice cold watermelon at Pontchartrain Beach in New Orleans, the world's most fragile pretzels at Willow Mill in Mechanicsburg, Pennsylvania, and butter-soaked roasting corn ears at Des Moines' Riverview Park are picnic memories that can be cherished forever. Corn on the cob may lack social acceptance by pinky-lifting gourmets, but as picnic fare it is unequaled.

The sound of someone biting into a crisp kosher pickle counterpointed by the roar of a roller coaster is music unmatched anywhere on earth. Eat your heart out, Beethoven! And have a little homemade chow-chow with your foot-long.

9: The Entertainments

Penny arcades are so popular that some amusement enterprises consist solely of coin-operated machines. These are not the sleezy kind found on metropolitan streets between pawn shops and burlesque shows, many of which have degenerated into hard-core porno peep shows, but solid operations where a whole family can have fun. Daytona Beach, Florida, for example, has two such operations: Joyland, a big, well-equipped penny arcade (with miniature golf on the roof), and the Mardi Gras Fun Center, a penny arcade combined with a restaurant.

Calling today's average arcade a penny arcade is as anachronistic as calling a 5″ hot dog a foot-long. But everybody does, and nobody gets mad. One of the three penny arcades operated at Santa Cruz Beach in California still has some 1¢ machines, but these are kept more for sentimental reasons than for anything else. Even the amusement devices considered old-time machines are nickel machines today, card machines are often a dime, and competitive games are two-players-for-a-quarter in most amusement parks.

As popular as penny arcades are in the United States, they are even more popular in England. Pleasure Beach in Blackpool has a dozen different penny arcades. So does Exhibition Park in Wembley, Middlesex, as well as having seven Bingo parlors. Europeans are strong on gambling devices. The Tivoli, in Copenhagen, Denmark, has Las Vegas-type slot machines plus 20 Wheels of Fortune.

Penny arcades in the United States had plenty of gambling devices at one time. Starting in 1886, the Mills Novelty Company of Chicago built slot machines of many ingenious kinds, including coin-operated roulette wheels, poker and blackjack rigs, dice games, and horse races. Indeed, as early as 1902, Mills's customers were in trouble with John Law, a problem Mills solved by adding a tinkling music cylinder and a notice on each machine reading: "Any person desiring to hear the music can do so by dropping a coin in the slot; as a consideration for the use of this machine and music furnished, it is agreed that any coins which may come out in the cup must and shall be played back into the machine for more music."

This particular notice is found on a machine that could handle ten players at a time and on machines that sometimes were built to take quarters, half-dollars, and even silver dollars—when a dollar was worth twenty-five times as much as it is today. But if the customers pocketed their winnings, after the manufacturer himself told them that they mustn't, it wasn't his fault if the device was regarded by some as a game of chance.

Originally, Herb Mills's primary business was building arcade equipment, such as fortune-telling machines, picture-viewing devices, and the like. But after Charles Fey of San Francisco invented the "modern" 3-reel slot machine in 1895, Mills built a similar machine, which grew so quickly in popularity that by 1907 the tail was wagging the dog. His four sons continued shipping the standard cherries-lemons-and-bells machines all over the world right up to World War II, when they went out of business.

Bally Manufacturing Company, today's leading builder of slot machines, as well as a supplier of pinball and skill arcade machines, still says with a straight face that a slot machine is only an amusement device. Maybe. But the slot machine is the only coin-operated device on which the federal government levies a

$250 tax per year, as does Clark County, Las Vegas. On top of that the State of Nevada whacks the owner with $40 tax each year. The owner of a Las Vegas slot machine is not overly concerned about the $540 per year nut; in a lively location his machine can make that in a week.

Slot machine profits are so enormous that the government of New South Wales in Australia collects an annual license fee, of up to $5,000 per machine, depending on the number of machines per location, plus a graduated tax on gross income, ranging from 12.5 to 24 percent—20¢ being the maximum denomination permitted for slot machine play. The owner of only half a dozen average slot machines in Nevada can net some $36,000 per year, according to tax collectors. Furthermore, the reported net profits on Nevada's 40,000 slot machines (the state takes a special 3 to 3.5 percent tax on gross win, depending on volume) hovers around $250 million per year.

Gambling games for the penny arcades were also made by Exhibit Supply Company of Chicago (ESCO), which was established in 1901 and became the world's largest manufacturer of amusement machines. ESCO's slot machine was purported to be a gumball dispenser, wherein lay its failure—it was too hard to keep filled up, and operators preferred the more forthright Mills machines. ESCO's dice machine was also a failure because it had a large pane of horizontal glass too tempting for too many losers, who smashed it with too much regularity.

ESCO's renown today is based on the Iron Claw machine, which has inspired any number of other digger machine imitations. The player manipulates the dangling cargo bucket, as on a freighter, over whatever prize he is trying for in the glass case. In a timed sequence, the claw comes down and closes around the prize, raises it, and swings it into the delivery chute.

Heavy or rounded prizes are wont to slip from the claw's grasp before getting to the chute, and crooked operators used to bolt the electric clocks and binoculars to the base, to improve the chances for the house even more. The average player would get two or three pieces of stale candy from the strewn base, but if he saw the claw actually move the prize he was after, he would be likely to play again and again and again. The Iron Claw was so popular at one time that whole truckloads of them traveled the carnival routes to serve as portable center joints.

ESCO also built some of the most innocuous gambling devices known to man. One was a penny version of the Bozo joint called Smiling Joe. Another was a vertical pinball cabinet. In both machines the player got a gum ball on each play, but if he shot his penny into the proper hole, he not only got the gum but got his penny back as well.

ESCO also built peep show machines, with motion produced by rapidly flipping cards. In those days watching a Flora Dora girl lift her skirt all the way to her knees really was quite a thrill. Some peep show machines, exhibiting only a series of still photographs that were considered quite daring at the time, could probably be used for Sunday school lessons today. But at the peak of their popularity, some penny arcades had entire lineups of these "spicy" eye-openers.

From peep show machines, ESCO got into building card vendors for the Straw Hats who wanted to take home more than a memory. Bathing girls, nymphs, and reigning burlesque queens of the period were all depicted on the cards. These vending machines got so much action that ESCO was soon producing more different kinds of card vendors than everybody else combined. The vastly popular cupid card would tell patrons who and when they would marry; the fortune-teller would advise on financial affairs; and for those whose tastes ran to palmistry or horoscopes, there were machines for them, too.

ESCO made 60 different kinds of card machines, and built up a selection of 3,500 different cards, including movie stars, prizefighters, and ball players. They printed so many cards (at a cost to the park of as little as $1.75 per thousand, as late as 1948) that they bought printing stock by the carload. Riverview Park alone bought 4.5 million cards one year.

Play on the card vending machines was so heavy, in fact, that John Franklin Meyer, the man most responsible for building up ESCO, developed an early version of S&H Green Stamps. Players who cut the prize corner off enough cards could receive—free!— such merchandise as boys' football equipment. However, they needed a lot of corners. Each prize corner had a hole in it, so the triangles could be strung together like so much wampum; a "string" was enough corners to measure 14 inches when tightly pressed together—and four strings were needed to get a football helmet.

Almost as well known as ESCO's card machines are its Meter Machines, each of which can electrically test the player's disposition, love potential, personality, glamour, sex appeal, or whatever. All the player has to do is squeeze two handles together and a light glows opposite the answer to his question. For a $30 machine cost, the parks got a popular machine that can take in that $30 in a good weekend—in pennies. And by golly, the player gets his penny's worth, too.

Another ESCO favorite is the coin-operated Hi-Striker. The player slams his fist down on the pad as hard as he can to see how high he can make the machine register. However, too many drunks missed the pad and broke their wrists or otherwise hurt themselves—which is why penny arcade Hi-Strikers are rare today. Similar strength-testers include the K-O Punch Machine, the Grip Tester, and a real hernia producer, the What-Can-You-Lift? Machine.

One of ESCO's most durable machines is the Learn-to-Shoot Machine. Players wield Luger-shaped mechanical pistols, affixed in swivels at the front of the glassed cabinet, and shoot steel ball bearings at a miniature shooting gallery. Some of these machines have been in use for almost half a century and are still more fun than much of the equipment in modern shooting galleries.

Many of today's penny arcades are full of electronic shooting devices, such as machine guns that shoot a ray of light at a moving electric eye on the glass surface of the back target. They are most often seen in parks that no longer have regular shooting galleries.

Shooting galleries using regulation .22 rifles with real ammunition are a thing of the past. Riverview had six separate shooting galleries around the park, until too many of the customers thought it was more fun to shoot at the lights on top of the Shoot-the-Chutes or, on occasion, to use the concessionaire's rifles for a holdup.

Today's best shooting galleries have BB rifles connected to an air compressor. The BB shot is steel, so that it will not be malformed, as would lead, when striking the backstop. Therefore it can be reused constantly. The clay pipes, once favored as targets, are no longer seen, and only a few old-time galleries still have iron candles with a gas-fed flame that only good marksmen can snuff out. Nevertheless the moving line of iron ducks remains, as do the jumping rabbits, hiding bears, and gong-centered bull's-eyes.

Playland at Rockaway Beach has five shooting galleries, and the one at Rye has two machine gun galleries (Rome's Luna Park has 21 shooting galleries). Ft. Markley Amusement Park in Seneca, Kansas, has a regulation rifle range, and Young's Park in Dickinson, North Dakota, has trap shooting. But the most challenging regular shooting gallery in the United States is at Lincoln Park in North Dartmouth, Massachusetts.

Although the fun house is not normally considered a concession, it's not a ride, either. Patrons are welcome to stay in the fun house and amuse themselves for as long as they like. Some of the lads used to hang around for hours in Aladdin's Castle at Riverview watching the girls who didn't know enough to hold their skirts down as they walked over hidden air jets.

One of the best fun houses in the United States is the German import on the Million Dollar Midway at State Fair Park in Dallas. Getting through the rolling barrel is too difficult for many patrons, so alongside there's an alternative walkway, but even *it* shakes. Other wierd walkways include one with wall-to-wall discs in the floor, rotating in opposite directions, one that operates like an escalator going the wrong way, and one called the Camel Back in which sections of the floor heave up and down.

Stairs that suddenly flatten out to become slides are more fun to watch than to walk on. So are tilting floors. The most difficult of all to navigate is the Anti-Gravity Room, where the entire room tilts and the furniture and fixtures remain parallel with the walls— stand in what you think is an upright posture, and you'll fall over.

The Spin-Out is another fun house entertainment for people who want to see how long they can resist centrifugal force as speed builds up in the 20-foot disc on which they sit. The "winner," who sits dead-center on the disc, gets so dizzy that he, too, is ultimately flung against the side wall. Back in the days when girls still wore skirts to amusement parks, watching the Spin-Out was one of the most popular spectator sports in the fun house.

Most fun houses have a Mirror Maze, in which the customers invariably get lost. This causes so much screaming that a Glass House is run as a separate attraction by some parks. And no fun house, anywhere, is complete without its Distorting Mirrors.

Steel Pier in Atlantic City has four fun houses, and Gaslight Village, Lake George, New York, has half a dozen. The Asians are even more demons for self-punishment—amusement parks such as Lai Chi Kok in Hong Kong have as many as 11 fun houses scattered throughout the grounds.

A Walk-Thru is related to the fun house insofar as the patron is self-ambulatory, but it offers only things to look at. The Walk-Thru also differs from a dark ride in that there is seldom any attempt to scare the patron. A Walk-Thru is often educational, featuring exhibits or animated displays related to a central theme. Mother Goose Land in Lolo, Montana, *is* a Walk-Thru, a full mile long. In Silver Springs, Florida, Six-Gun Territory has 40 Walk-Thrus for people who want to take a rest from the rides.

Nowadays, when just about everybody is considered some kind of a freak, the sideshow, with its Bearded Lady, Tattooed Man, and Jo-Jo, the Dog-Faced Boy, is seldom seen in amusement parks. Riverview had the largest aggregation of strange-looking human beings in North America at one time, but most freak shows today are carnival operations because so many of them are fakes.

In contrast, straight variety shows are more popular today than ever. Pirate's World in Dania, Florida, which is a better amusement park than the name would indicate, puts on full-scale musical comedy productions. Grand opera at Whalom Park in Massachusetts, symphony concerts at Hersheypark in Pennsylvania, and recitals by some of the world's leading musicians at Elitch's Gardens in Colorado often are outstanding, as are any number of plays at the many summer theaters operated by amusement parks around the country. The Miss America Contest in Atlantic City, of course, gets worldwide television and press coverage, and just about every major park in the country runs bathing beauty contests and talent contests of one kind or another, such as the ones held at the 4,500-seat theater at Chilhowee Park in Knoxville. Griffen Amusement Park in Jacksonville, Florida, has an impressive Spring Band Festival every year. Some of the most delightful entertainments anywhere are the puppet shows at Dandilion Park, Muskego, Wisconsin. The theme parks, of course, led by the Disney, Opryland, and Six Flags operations, all feature musical shows, strolling minstrels, street entertainment, simulated cowboy shoot-outs, stagecoach holdups, train robberies, and Indian raids.

And then there are the animal acts, most of the best ones coming from Animal Behavior Enterprises in Hot Springs, Arkansas, which are proliferating everywhere. The late Keller Breland's ABE trained the porpoises now at Marine World in California, the macaws at Parrot Jungle in Florida, and the piano-playing pig, Pigerace, at Opryland. Breland's widow, Marian, now ships out animal acts to amusement parks all over the world, including trained dogs, cats, chickens, ducks, raccoons, rabbits, and seals. The rabbit who plays the piano for the dancing chicken will not only accept a tip but also put it in his piggy bank. The horseshoe-playing polly also roller skates—and is pretty good at it. Remarkably, all these animals seem to enjoy showing off their smarts. Matching wits with an educated chicken can be almost traumatic, particularly when the chicken cackles its delight after winning a quiz. Mrs. Breland's porpoises have the biggest grins of any hams in show biz.

Aside from talented animals, scores of amusement parks maintain a private zoo, especially in towns that do not have municipal menageries. One of the best is at Legend City in Tempe, Arizona, which has a zoo where all the denizens are exclusively desert animals. A petting and feeding zoo is popular at any amusement park, and not just with children. The Japanese Village in Buena Park, California, has 400 tame deer on the grounds, including some of the fattest in the land. Southwick Park, Mendon, Massachusetts, offers elephant rides instead of the traditional pony rides.

The ballroom has been a feature at every major park in the country since the last century, although there isn't much ballroom dancing anymore. Buckeye Lake Park in Ohio has three such edifices.

Most skating rinks don't get much play anymore, either, although ice and roller rinks are still maintained by many of the older parks.

Two exceptions are found in the Chicago area. The Adventureland and Santa's Village amusement parks in the western suburbs are the direct outgrowth of an ice-skating rink called Rainbow Arena in Chicago.

Many amusement parks hang onto special side attractions long after they have gone out of date. Buck Lake in Angola, Indiana, still puts on wrestling matches, even though everybody else in the country knows what "put on" really means. Then there are the patrons who use the trampolines at Cascade Park, New Castle, Pennsylvania. Apparently they don't know or don't care that such devices have been junked long ago by most former operators. Go-Kart tracks may be dead just about everywhere else, but not at Playland in Salina, Kansas. They're still pitching horseshoes at Northern Woods in Carmel, Indiana. Kishacoquillas Park in Lewistown, Pennsylvania, still doggedly features slot car racing.

Miniature golf, another goner in most other kinds of amusement areas, is still big in amusement parks all over the country. Joyland, in Decatur, Indiana, has a full 36-hole layout. Driving ranges for golfers are also big. Hoffman's Playland in Newtonville, New York, gets such heavy play that a double-deck driving range had to be built to take care of the volume. Pitch & Putt (Par 3) courses get a lot of action, too; the one at Sandy Lake Park in Dallas is surprisingly tough. Some amusement parks also operate regulation 18-hole golf links in conjunction with more common attractions. The course maintained by Stone Mountain Park, Stone Mountain, Georgia, is one of the most challenging golf courses anywhere.

Bowling alleys have been built into a number of amusement parks, too. Although Celebrity Center in Denver has a penny arcade and a shooting gallery, it's not a real amusement park because there isn't room—but it has 80 bowling lanes. Baseball is also into the amusement park picture, not just because of the provisions at many athletic fields within the park grounds, but also because of the automated batting practice machines, such as at Funland in Thomson, Illinois. Ping-pong courts have been growing in popularity ever since President Nixon got back from China; Foothill Park, La Crescenta, California, has four of them.

Numerous amusement parks have been built at beaches, where the main attraction is the bathing rather than the rides. Coney Island probably couldn't hang on at all if it wasn't for the swimming. Many parks not on a natural shoreline, and some that are, build swimming pools, which get heavy patronage.

About the ultimate in providing all means of pleasure for their customers are the amusement parks that have motels right on the premises. The Casino Pier, Seaside Heights, New Jersey; Crystal Beach, Elizabethtown, North Carolina; Indiana Beach, Monticello, Indiana; and Pera's Amusement Park, Geneva-on-the-Lake, Ohio, do a lot to support the contention that amusement parks are primarily *not* for kids.

Such pleasure — and for only a penny!

...ly advertisement for penny ...ade equipment.

...Old-fashioned penny arcade with its ...assortment of peep shows.

...e dismal penny arcade attracted ... patrons to Palisades Park in ...w Jersey (photo taken in March ...2).

Lincoln Park (North Dartmouth, Massachusetts) features this version of the popular shooting gallery.

The freak show as a feature of amusement park midways has almost disappeared.

Fun houses are not always as extravagant as Mountain Park's Outer Space (Holyoke, Massachusetts).

Two of the more surprising talented animals trained by Animal Behavior Enterprises.

Part 4

TRADITIONAL AMUSEMENT
PARKS~STILL HANGING IN THERE

This section includes ratings ranging from 4-star parks (★★★★), which are considered among the best in the country, down to 1-star parks (★), which means that they have serious limitations.

Evaluations are based on concept, design, and variety of the rides and attractions; safety; maintenance of the grounds; cleanliness; degree of con; personnel; type of patronage; prices; and in general, just how much plain fun they are to go to.

Listings are in the order of size, judged by the number of major rides. Special attractions and features are enumerated.

10: New York

Coney Island is to the amusement park industry what Hollywood is to the movie industry. The average American who has never been to Brooklyn thinks that Coney Island *is* an amusement park, but it's not; it simply happens to be where a lot of individual amusement parks are operated on a one-mile stretch along the ocean in South Brooklyn.

Coney Island, which used to be infested with wild rabbits, or coneys, is an island in name only. The old tidal creek that separated it from the rest of Brooklyn was filled in many years ago. Geographically, the sandbar called Coney Island includes Brighton Beach (named for the famous resort in England), a densely populated year-round residential community to the east. Beyond Brighton are Manhattan and Oriental Beaches, with some of the best bathing beaches on the Atlantic Ocean. Surf Avenue, Coney Island's main thoroughfare, separates the amusement area from the drab community to the north.

The great Steeplechase Park building, which George Tilyou erected so that the rides could operate regardless of the weather during the short New York season, is gone. Its old reflecting pool is now a parking lot. The parachute drop, moved to Coney Island from the New York World's Fair of 1939, is an abandoned eyesore, and the city would be delighted to *give* it to anybody willing to remove it. The land on which the Cyclone roared for so many years, at the east end of Coney Island, was bought by the New York Aquarium after the Cyclone's last season, in 1973.

Coney Island still has an operation called Steeplechase Park, but today it consists of a mere dozen or so rides, all outdoors. To the east, the Wonder Wheel still dazzles visitors, and Astroland next door not only does capacity business on its now 10-year-old Space Tower, soaring some 300 feet over Brooklyn, but is still adding new rides every year.

Happily, Coney Island isn't dead by a long shot. The crowds still pour out of the Stillwell Avenue subway terminal all summer long, mostly seeking relief from the heat of the city's streets. The Empire of the Nickel may have raised its prices and lowered its standards, but as long as that cooling beach remains on the other side of the boardwalk, Coney Island will always be in business.

Twelve miles to the east, just below Kennedy Airport, is an amusement park quite similar to the parks at Coney Island— Playland at Rockaway Beach in Queens. But it stands alone in cramped quarters, solidly surrounded by a typical residential neighborhood. Its old-fashioned Rocket is one of the few such flat rides left, its fun house is one of the best in the country, and the Hell 'n Back dark ride is second to none. Much of Rockaway's success is due to Richard L. Geist, one of the best promoters in the business. The park was built in 1901 by L. A. Thompson, of Scenic Railways fame, and some of the original equipment is still in use. Rockaway's Playland probably has more action per minute per square foot than any other amusement park in the United States.

New York's other Playland, across Long Island Sound at Rye, Westchester County, is the biggest amusement park in the state. Owned and operated by the county, it is the world's largest facility of its kind operated by a government authority. The park covers some 200 acres, about half of which is given over to the aging rides and attractions. The other half is under environmental maintenance: woodlands, gardens, a scenic lake, and even a wild bird sanctuary.

Westchester County traditionally has sported impressive homes, luxuriant lawns, and an air of well-groomed opulence. Thus, when, during the 1920s, the burghers of Rye saw the development of a tawdry, commercial amusement park in their midst, they deplored it as a "disreputable and honky-tonk operation" and petitioned the county to rehabilitate the site. During the proceedings, the ill-regarded Paradise Park burned to the ground, and the result is the recently rebuilt Playland, orginally opened in 1928, and now one of the newest, old-time parks around.

Some of Rye's kiddieland equipment was originally used by kids who now bring their grandchildren to go on the same rides. The colonnades, pavilions, and buildings are beautifully kept up, but it is still obvious that they were built during the era of Herbert Hoover. The best ride in the park is the Big Dragon roller coaster, which Mayor Jimmy Walker once chartered for an entire afternoon for the exclusive use by himself and his pals.

The best amusement park for upstate New Yorkers is actually not in New York but across the river from Buffalo, in Ontario, Canada. With the addition of new equipment, installed in the early 1970s, Crystal Beach, which has always had more games than Rye and has a Fantasy Land for the kids, as well as slot car racing for the kids who have forgotten that they are growing up, now has more major rides. The paved and landscaped Million Dollar Midway is a mile long, and a truly beautiful picnic grove has facilities for 5,000 people, including seven new covered picnic pavilions. Crystal Beach is one of the really great parks, but it may have to change its name if by "crystal" they refer to the waters of Lake Erie.

Sea Breeze Amusement Park in Rochester is now owned by George Long, the eminent merry-go-round horse carver. Opening day was August 5, 1879, when the Rochester & Lake Ontario Street Railway began running. The first ride was the 1903 Figure

Storytown U.S.A., Lake George, New York, is one of the most heavily patronized amusement parks in the state.

Steeplechase Park as it appeared in its heyday.

The heart of modern Coney Island.

Rockaway's Playland still sports some of the original equipment built for the park's opening in 1901.

...ayland in Rye, New York, features this magnificent ...e Casino.

Eight roller coaster, and George Long's father put in the merry-go-round the following year. During the 1920s, Sea Breeze had as many as four roller coasters at one time,· but after the Great Depression hit, the traction company came to Long and asked if he would like to take over the park on a rental basis. As soon as he did, he tried to rename the park Dreamland in emulation of the Coney Island razzle-dazzle of the same name. However, everybody still calls the park Sea Breeze, including all the people who work there. By the mid 1940s, Sea Breeze was recognized as one of the major parks in the country, and it still is.

Joe Schuler, owner of a second amusement park in Rochester, Olympic Park, is proudest of his 3-train miniature railroad, which runs on a full one-mile track. Counting his 14 kiddie rides, Schuler actually has more rides in his 28-ride total than George Long, plus a golf driving range, roller rink, and bowling alley. He finally gave up Go-Karts as a lost cause in 1972.

By virtue of being within the Adirondack Forest Preserve, Lake George is one of the most heavily patronized amusement areas in the state. The small town has two separate amusement parks, and both big ones. True, they are theme parks, but only halfheartedly so. Storytown U.S.A. has not just one but many themes—plus 15 major rides and as good a penny arcade as can be found anywhere. Gaslight Village has six fun houses along with ten major rides, penny arcade, and shooting gallery.

Glen Park Actionland in Williamsville tries to sound wicked with its Inferno Lounge, but the park remains most noted for its kiddie rides and excellent zoo.

Kaydeross Park, Sarasota Springs, is the place to go for the best grab joints in the state; the park has not just hot dogs but clam bakes and even steak roasts all season.

When bellies are full and the flashing lights begin to hurt the eyes rather than dazzle, the last ride before going home is always the merry-go-round, to leave on just the right note. At Nunley's, in Baldwin, even the merry-go-round horses look sleepy by closing time.

PARKS IN NEW YORK

★★★★Buffalo—Crystal Beach Park (actually in Ontario, Canada). Features beach, roller rink, ballroom, pony track, Fantasy Land, wax museum, slot car racetrack, miniature golf, athletic fields, picnic facilities, orchestras, free acts, fireworks.

★★Rye—Playland. Owned by Westchester County. Features pool, beach, ice rink, miniature golf, driving range, athletic fields, pony track, boat rentals, picnic facilities, firewoorks.

★★★★Rochester—Dreamland Park (also known as Sea Breeze). Features miniature golf, picnic facilities, merry-go-round horses carved by park owner, George Long.

★Flushing—Adventure Amusement Park. Features fun house.

★★Rochester—Olympic Park. Features zoo, miniature golf, driving range, baseball batting range, bowling, billiards, Go-Karts, picnic facilities, fireworks.

★★Brooklyn (Coney Island)—Steeplechase Park. Features baseball batting range, beach, pony track, picnic facilities, free acts, fireworks in weak simulation of the original.

★Manlius—Suburban Park. Features fun house, ballroom, miniature golf, athletic field, picnic facilities.

★★★★Rockaway Beach—Rockaway's Playland. Features fun house, beach, miniature golf, adjacent to publicly owned athletic field, picnic facilities, beauty contests, excursion boats, fireworks.

★★★Canandaigua—Roseland Park. Features fun house, miniature golf, slot car racetrack, athletic field, picnic facilities, concerts at Roseland Bowl.

★Elmira—Eldridge Park. City owned. Features athletic fields, miniature golf, theater, picnic facilities, orchestras, bands. Free acts, fireworks on Sundays.

★★★Brooklyn (Coney Island)—Astroland. Features fun house.

★Brooklyn—Steeplechase Park. Features baseball batting range, pony track, beach, picnic facilities. Resembles George Tilyou's Steeplechase Park—both located in the same neighborhood of Coney Island.

★★Tioga Center—Skyline Amusement Park. Features fun house, miniature golf, athletic field, picnic facilities, free acts, fireworks.

★East Farmingdale—Adventureland. Features photo booths, sidewalk-type artists.

★★West Webster—Willow Point Park. Features ballroom, roller rink, miniature golf, driving range, baseball batting range, trampolines, Ping-Pong, athletic field, picnic facilities, orchestras, name bands.

★★Caroga Lake—Sherman's Amusement Park. Features ballroom, beach, marina, zoo, athletic field, picnic facilities, orchestras, vaudeville, free acts, fireworks.

★★Maple Springs—Midway Park. Features roller rink, miniature golf, athletic field, picnic facilities, fireworks.

★★★Saratoga Springs—Kaydeross Park. Features clam bakes, steak roasts, swimming pool, beach, ballroom, sailing club, waterskiing shows.

★★Waverly—Fraley's Amusement Park. Features ballroom, miniature golf, picnic facilities, orchestras, free acts.

★★Ferndale—Fun-Fare Amusement Park. Features swinging gym, roller rink, Go-Karts, animal farm, saddle horses, miniature golf, driving range with a pro, picnic facilities, orchestras.

★★Genesco—Long Point Park. Features beach, roller rink, athletic field, picnic facilities.

★Tonawanda—Fun-N-Games. Features miniature golf, driving range, relatively new overgrown kiddieland, fireworks.

★★Olcott—New Rialto Park. Features fun house, picnic facilities.

★Olcott—Olcott Beach Park. Features beach, picnic facilities.

★★★Binghamton—Airport Kiddieland. Features miniature golf, picnic facilities, free acts for special events.

★Williamsville—Glen Park Actionland. Features ballroom, zoo, Inferno Lounge, picnic facilities, orchestras, vaudeville, free acts.

★★Brooklyn—Fairyland Kiddie Park.

★Binghampton—Ross Park. Features miniature golf, zoo, picnic facilities.

11: New Jersey

ATLANTIC City is second only to Coney Island as the most famous amusement area in the United States. Primarily built to serve the Philadelphia-Camden market, it is an outright amusement factory, operated as if on a mass-production, assembly-line system, with the boardwalk as its conveyor belt.

The boardwalk in Atlantic City is unique. Sixty feet wide for much of its 4-mile length, it is built of steel and concrete, overlaid with pine planking in a herringbone pattern (20 miles of planks are used every year just for maintenance). Atlantic City Rolling Chairs, invented there in 1884, have accommodated uncounted millions of sight-seeing visitors as they have been trundled along the boardwalk; some of the manually pushed models are almost as wide as davenports.

The picture postcard also was introduced to America, in 1895, in Atlantic City, as was salt water taffy, which gets its name by association rather than from the ingredients.

Amusement piers, almost as characteristic of Atlantic City as the boardwalk, were built on the same principle as the skyscraper, except that they are horizontal, thereby occupying little space on the boardwalk but packing as much amusement behind the entrances as possible.

The 2,000-foot Steel Pier is currently the longest pier on the boardwalk, with room enough for four theaters, four fun houses, and a couple of good restaurants. It's not much for rides, but it puts on the best beauty contests in the country, Bert Parks included. It also has more attractions for children than most other Atlantic City operations, including a good-sized Ferris wheel with closed gondolas.

Now less than a third of its original length due to three fires, Central Pier was once Atlantic City's longest pier, (2,700 feet stretching out into the Atlantic Ocean for more than half a mile). However, it still is the most fun on the boardwalk, with some 200 hanky-panks on the premises. In addition, it has half-a-dozen good rides, three fun houses, and an excellent penny arcade; it even sports a Space Tower.

An investment of $1 million in an amusement park doesn't mean much these days, and the Million Dollar Pier shows it. Built in 1906, the pier now is showing its age. Most of the dozen rides currently operating are pretty creaky, all too many of the venerable machines in the penny arcade are inoperable, and the Italian Village is a bore. The little Ferris wheel is too small to get much action, and it is closed down much of the time.

Because the gulf stream comes close enough to temper Atlantic City's winter climate, a surprising number of steady visitors use it as a winter resort, though most of the winter population are the retired, who sun themselves on the boardwalk while prudently wearing overcoats. In any case, there aren't enough winter visitors to warrant operating the rides, and the deserted piers are eerie as the waves lap against the pilings under the silent rides. You can almost feel the cables rusting above the empty Sky Ride cars. In short, winter on the piers is a whole spooky world apart from the gaiety of the summer season, when there might be half a million people on the frenetic boardwalk.

Contrary to popular opinion, the best rides in New Jersey are not in Atlantic City but rather down at the tip of the state, at the

Wildwood complex. The exceptionally wide Marine Pier, built mostly over dry land, is updated yearly.

Farther up the coast at Seaside Heights, the Casino & Pier operation also maintains a steady program of improvements, but the service at the hotel and restaurants is deplorable and the prices are way out of line. Perhaps this is because it can rely on a New York market more than amusement parks farther south. At Seaside Park, Funtown U.S.A. even overcharges the kids in what is one of the state's biggest kiddielands. Funtown's Sky Ride is another gyp—just barely clearing the roofs of the concessions.

Two of the many faces of Atlantic City's Boardwalk.

Aerial view of Funtown, U.S.A., Seaside Heights, New Jersey.

PARKS IN NEW JERSEY

★★★Wildwood—Wildwood Marine Pier. Features miniature golf.

★Seaside Heights—Seaside Heights Casino & Pier. Features night clubs, pool, beach, fishing pier, ballroom, miniature golf, athletic field, picnic facilities, hotel on the premises, orchestras, name bands, vaudeville, free acts.

★Seaside Park—Funtown U.S.A. Features fun houses, beach, free acts.

★Clementon—Clementon Lake Park. Features fun houses, beach, miniature golf, athletic field, picnic facilities, fireworks.

★★Mt. Arlington—Bertrand Park. Features fun house, beach, ballroom, miniature golf, athletic field, picnic facilities.

★★Wildwood—Sportland Pier. Features swimming pool, slides, beach, motordrome, trampolines, bicycle rentals, Aqua Circus.

★Wildwood—Fun Pier. Features fun houses, minature golf, beach.

★Atlantic City—Million Dollar Pier. Features beach, Italian Village.

★Ocean City—Wonderland Pier. Relatively new.

★Point Pleasant—Point Pleasant Pavillion. Features fun house, beach, miniature golf.

★★Asbury Park—Palace Amusements. Features fun house.

★★Wildwood—Casino Arcade Park. Features miniature gold, tram trains.

★★★★Atlantic City—Central Pier. Features fun houses, miniature golf, aquarium, Space Tower.

★Point Pleasant Beach—Ocean Amusement Rides. Features bathing beach.

★★Beverly—Olympia Lakes. Features swimming pool, beach, ballroom, miniature golf, athletic field, picnic facilities, orchestras, name bands, free acts.

★★Belmar—Belmar Playland. Features swimming pool, beach picnic facilities, name bands, free acts. Relatively new.

★★★Atlantic City—Steel pier. Features fun houses, ballroom, picnic facilities, beauty contests, circuses, television shows, first-run movies, children's theater, name bands, vaudeville.

★★Ocean City—Playland. Features fun house, beach.

★★Mays Landing—Lenape Park Recreation Center. Features beach, miniature golf, athletic field, picnic facilities.

★Long Branch—Recreation Pier. Features pool, beach, miniature golf, racetrack, boating, picnic facilities, fireworks.

★★Bayonne—Bergen Point Amusement Park. Features fun house, miniature golf, orchestras, fireworks.

Seaside Heights—Freeman's Amusement Center. Not quite an amusement park in the strict sense, but has one of the best old-world Merry-Go-Rounds in North America.

12: New England

Amusement parks in New England are strong on dark rides, fun houses, and Walk-Thrus. For example, the traditional fun house at Lincoln Park, North Dartmouth, Massachusetts, has served as a model for many others around the country, and has a thousand fun makers for "laffs and thrills," including one of the most baffling Mirror Mazes anywhere.

Riverside Park in Agawam, Massachusetts, has a fun house modeled after the famous Oktoberfest building in Munich, Germany, with over two dozen separate attractions. Riverside also has a Lost River Ride through "darkest Africa" complete with headhunters. The Castle of Terror at Rocky Point Park, Warwick, Rhode Island, purports to be so frightening that the management maintains a fake nurse in attendance to revive the faint-hearted.

Many kids actually breathe a sigh of relief as their cars emerge from Paragon Park's Kooky Kastle at Nantasket Beach, Massachusetts, but they always go back for more. One dark ride at Mountain Park in Holyoke, Massachusetts, is unique in that the cars pop out and over the midway after being menaced by animated dinosaurs and man-eaters. Mountain Park's Out of This

130

World, which is even more scary, is a journey into outer space, full of horrible little green men from Mars, shooting stars, meteors that just barely miss the moving spaceships, and berserk robots that threaten to kidnap everybody forever.

Whalom Park's dark ride in Lunnenburg, Massachusetts, the Pirate's Den, is frightening enough to scare a real pirate—excellent for producing chills on a hot summer's day. At Canobie Lake Park, Salem, New Hampshire, the patron has a choice between protecting himself from bats in The House of Seven Gables or getting lost among the snakes and alligators in The Swamp. (Rather than make a choice, go through both. And don't miss the separate Mirror Maze.)

Most of Canobie Lake Park's 175 acres is used for picnic groves, which include a pavilion as well as barbeque pits and fireplaces. There's also a big athletic field with a ball park, horseshoe pitching pits, and a podium. At the opposite end of the park is an excellent swimming pool. Still more of the grounds are used for a ballroom, a roller rink, bowling alleys, a restaurant, and a big boat house (excursion boats for lake cruises are featured, as well as speedboat rentals). Though there's no miniature railroad, there is a track for pumper-type handcars, something unique in the East. Even more land is used for two separate tracks for junior sports cars and antique-looking Tin Lizzies. The inevitable kiddieland is pretty big, too.

But what room is left is used for one of the best midways on the eastern seaboard. Canobie Lake has not just one merry-go-round, but three. The really big roller coaster is supplemented with a Galaxi and a junior version for little kids. Flat rides include one of the last Caterpillars left in America, as well as the venerable Flying Scooter, Tilt-a-Whirl, and Whip, plus the more mundane Calypso, Roundup, Crazy Cups, and Helicopter rides. There are also a Flying Missile, a Cosmo Jet, and a Merry Mixer. Skee Ball and the Dodgem cars have separate buildings.

Canobie's penny arcade even has machines that still operate for a penny. A good balance of hanky-panks includes many play-'till-you-win games. The grounds are studded with refreshment stands, not to mention rest rooms and drinking fountains, rarities in many amusement parks. Over it all swings a spectacular Sky Ride.

The equipment is excellently maintained; the grounds are clean without being fastidious; and the personnel are pleasant. Canobie Lake Park draws some trade from Massachusetts, but if it were closer to a big city the owners would be multi-millionaires.

In fact, Canobie Lake Park is one of the two best parks in general in all of New England—all the more impressive because it is the only traditional amusement park in the entire state. Even without any competition, it wouldn't have to be nearly as good as it is, but apparently Anthony Berni, Claude Captell, and Kas Ulaky *like* the amusement park business. Their park deserves a close look.

New England's biggest park is Agawam's Riverside Park, with 28 major rides, a monorail overhead train, and the El Dorado Mine Train, which goes to a Pioneer Main Street of the Old West. The old Water Sled Ride, the last Shoot-the-Chutes in New England, doesn't operate anymore, but the Thunderbolt is still running from April to September. However, like just about everything else in the park, it is a bit oversold—it does not go anywhere near the 60 mph claimed for it. Riverside is operated in conjunction with the Great Barrington Fairgrounds, which also draws huge crowds to the stock car racetrack.

Paragon Park in Hull, Massachusetts, runs a close second to Riverside in size—and its rides are better. Paragon's roller coaster doesn't go any 60 mph either, but it is considerably faster and better designed for thrills than either of Ed Carroll's two coaster rides. Paragon also has a watered-down version of the Chutes.

The best merry-go-round in New England, considering even the music, is at Lake Quassapaug Amusement Park in Middlebury, Connecticut. It's only a 3-abreast, but the hand-carved horses are beautiful. The only other merry-go-round that can compete with it in New England is the Looff-carved old-timer at Crescent Park in Riverside, Rhode Island.

Breathtaking roller coaster at Paragon Park (Hull, Massachusetts).

One of the many attractions at Riverside Park in Agawam, Massachusetts, is its fun house.

The Castle of Terror is one of 27 rides at Rocky Point Park in Warwick, Rhode Island.

The oldest park in New England is Lake Compounce in Bristol, Connecticut. It has the only big roller coaster left in the state.

PARKS IN NEW ENGLAND

MAINE

★★Old Orchard Beach—Palace Playland. Features fun house, beach, roller rink, racetrack, zoo, ballroom.

NEW HAMPSHIRE

★★★★Salem—Canobie Lake Park. Features fun house, swimming pool, sunning beach, roller rink, ballroom, athletic field, miniature golf, picnic facilities, lake cruises, speedboats, races, record hops, orchestras, name bands, vaudeville, free acts, fireworks.

MASSACHUSETTS

★★Agawam—Riverside Park. Features roller rink, miniature golf, athletic field, picnic facilities, auto racing stadium, orchestras, vaudeville, free acts, fireworks.

★★★Hull—Paragon Park. Features beach, miniature golf, picnic facilities, free acts, fireworks.

★★North Dartmouth—Lincoln Park. Features fun houses, roller rink, bowling, ballroom, miniature golf, driving range, zoo, athletic field, picnic facilities, orchestras, name bands, free acts, fireworks.

★★★Holyoke—Mountain Park. Features fun houses, ballroom, miniature golf, athletic field, picnic facilities, summer stock theater, name bands, orchestras, vaudeville, free acts, fireworks.

★★★Lunenburg—Whalom Park. Features fun house, beach, roller rink, miniature golf, bowling alleys, motor launches, athletic field, picnic facilities.

★Boston—Revere Beach. Features fun house, racetrack, beach, miniature golf, picnic facilities, free acts, fireworks.

★Salisbury Beach—Shaheen's Fun-O-Rama Park. Features miniature golf, fireworks.

★★Mendon—Lake View Amusement Park. Features beach, ballroom, nightclub, athletic field, picnic facilities, orchestras, name bands, fireworks.

★★★Salem Willows—Salem Willows Park. Owned by Salem Willows Merchants Association. Features fun house, beaches, miniature golf, athletic field, picnic facilities, boating, fishing, harbor excursions, yacht club, public boat landing, fireworks.

★North Attleboro—Jolly Cholly Funland. Features miniature golf, picnic facilities.

★★Hull—Funland Park. Features beach, nightclub, marina, orchestras.

★Salisbury Beach—Nat's Salisbury Beach Fun Spot. Features baseball batting range, miniature golf, driving range, archery range, Go-Karts, Moon Walk.

★★Dracut—Lakeview Park. Features beach, athletic field, picnic facilities, free acts, fireworks.

CONNECTICUT

★★New London—Ocean Beach Park. City owned. Features cocktail lounges, ballroom, miniature golf, saltwater pool, beach, picnic facilities, free acts, fireworks.

★★★★Bristol—Lake Compounce. Oldest amusement park in the

United States. Features ballroom, miniature golf, beach, athletic field, picnic facilities, orchestras, free acts, fireworks.

★Middlebury—Lake Quassapaug Amusement Park. Features miniature golf, ballroom, beach, athletic field, picnic facilities, free acts, fireworks.

RHODE ISLAND

★★Warwick—Rocky Point Park. Features pool, beach, ballroom, miniature golf, athletic field, picnic facilities, zoo, motor launch, docking facilities, ferry service, orchestras, name bands, free acts, fireworks.

★★★Riverside—Crescent Park. Features fun house, ballroom, miniature golf, cocktail lounge, athletic field, picnic facilities, orchestras, name bands, free acts, fireworks.

★Providence—Roger Williams Park. Owned by the city. Features athletic field, picnic facilities, zoo, floral displays, museum, fireworks.

★★Misquamicut—Atlantic Beach Casino. Features beach, roller rink, athletic field, miniature golf, picnic facilities, orchestras.

13: Pennsylvania

In attitudes, Pennsylvania is a United States in miniature. It is sophisticated in the east, relaxed in the west, hard-working in the north, and dignified in the south.

Western Pennsylvania has one of the heaviest concentrations of amusement parks in the country. Half a dozen serve the Pittsburgh area alone, including the biggest park in the state—Kennywood.

This sprawling old park was built in 1898 by the Monongahela Street Railways Company, and Andrew H. Mellon thought enough of it to hire such luminaries as John Philip Sousa to attract the crowds riding the open-air summer trolleys. The original bandstand burned down in 1961, but there's a new and bigger showcase, called Starvue, for today's television and movie stars.

Counting more than a dozen kiddie rides, Kennywood has 46 rides, including one of the few double-track roller coasters extant. The Turnpike Ride, with miniature sports cars running over a guidance rail, is unique in America, as is the vastly popular Noah's Ark. But Kennywood is dragging its feet, and the best thing it has going for it is its midway of old-time hanky-panks, where you can still "test your strength and ring the bell" on the old Hi-Striker.

Some 45 miles to the east at Ligonier, is Idlewild, a much smaller but prettier park. Idlewild, too, was started by Mellon interests, and although it is about twenty years older than Kennywood, it's in better shape today. Its dozen or so major rides, upgraded every season, are set in some of the most carefully tended gardens in the state. The wooded areas have more than 800 picnic tables, with free firewood for the stone fireplaces.

People from all over the country bring their tots to see Idlewild's famous Story Book Forest, a separate 17-acre section where costumed people tell outrageous lies about giants, empty cupboards, and shoe-type housing for the impecunious elderly. During the one-hour tour, the luckier tykes may share a cookie with Little Red Riding Hood on the way to Grandma's house. The Three Little Pigs and Bambi are among the many live animals who live in Story Book Forest. Kids under 59 inches in height get in for half price.

Regardless of how good business is, Idlewild is closed Mondays, except on holidays. And as the management puts it, "Temperance is strictly enforced," which means that no beer, wine, or liquor is allowed on the grounds. Idlewild may be a bit stuffy, but it *is* beautiful.

Amusement parks in northern Pennsylvania, such as Waldameer Park in Erie and Nay Aug Park in Scranton, tend to be smaller, noisier, and dirtier—not that a little untidiness necessarily keeps an amusement park from being a good one. Dorney Park, in the eastern part of the state at Allentown, has some of the sloppiest groundskeepers in the business, but nevertheless it is a genuinely fun park.

Dorney is one of the few traditional amusement parks with an affectionately recognized symbolic clown. The animated 20-foot Alfundo, residing over the main gate, greets visitors as they enter. As the guiding spirit of the park, Alfundo is credited with everybody's having a good time. He is listed as editor of the park's house organ and gets blamed when the garbage cans start to overflow. It was Alfundo, legend says, who established the policy of free rides for all on the 90-year-old merry-go-round.

The park is owned and operated by the Dorney Park Coaster Company, which was founded in 1884 by a dedicated roller coaster buff, the grandfather of Bob Ott, today's third-generation president and general manager. As is proper, Dorney's huge roller coaster is rated as one of the best in America.

In the 1960s, Dorney was selected by Columbia Pictures as *the* typical American amusement park, and part of a Rosalind Russell movie was filmed there. The park does have, however, such untypical features as a racetrack and a full-fledged zoo, with everything up to and including a polar bear, giraffe, and hippopotamus.

The Inn at Dorney is famous for white Pekin duck dinners, and the climax of each season is the Labor Day weekend Apple Butter Festival with Pennsylvania Dutch cooking, arts and crafts, and entertainment. This is the real stuff, too, and not like the fakery in the theme parks exploiting the Amish around Lancaster.

One park in the Pennsylvania Dutch country, in the southern part of the state, that does not exploit the territory is Hersheypark, the big old park owned by the chocolate company in its own company town. Currently, the park is in the most ambitious expansion program of any traditional amusement park in the country.

The truly great merry-go-round (16 massive outside horses, 8 smaller inside stationary horses, 42 jumpers, and 2 chariots), used for many years at Coney Island and now the oldest still in use in America, has been moved to a major focal point called Carrousel Circle. The lines of people wait in an air-conditioned area. As another convenience, a tram service carries patrons to and from the parking lots.

In addition, the park has a new English Tudor Square, a 1,000-seat Aqua Theater, animal gardens, Deutsch Platz, and Rhine Land. With the construction of an Indian Village, Tower Plaza (a contemporary area), and a Pennsylvania Coal Mining Town in 1974, the New England Fishing Village in 1975, and the Frontier Town in 1976, the 62-acre grounds will have a complex of theme parks second to none in excellence (7 acres bigger than

Hershey Park as it appeared in 1916.

Idlewild Park in Ligonier, Pennsylvania, has some of the most carefully tended gardens in the state.

Idlewild Park's Story Book Forest attracts many youngsters who listen attentively to the costumed characters' tales.

Conneaut Lake Park enjoys a lively trade on it midway.

Conneaut Lake Park operates an authentic steam locomotive, formerly owned by the Grand Trunk and Western Railroad. It is believed to be the only still-operating locomotive built during World War I for the U.S. Railroad Administration.

Kennywood Park in West Mifflin, Pennsylvania, features the unique and popular Noah's Ark.

California's Disneyland). Hersheypark already offers a one-price policy for those who prefer it to the general admission plan.

Hersheypark was a big-time operation long before the name was spelled as one word. The ballroom has known such greats as Guy Lombardo, Sammy Kaye, Rudy Vallee, Paul Whiteman, Stan Kenton, Harry James, and Vaughn Monroe. Ben Hogan was the pro for many years on the golf course. The private zoo is so big that it is open the year around as a municipal service.

The penny arcade is one of the most complete in the country, but Hersheypark has always been unique for a traditional park in that there are no hanky-panks, except for a couple of super-honest ball games. Manager John Hart explains that it is important to the park to have a reputation for a quiet atmosphere with no pressure on visitors to spend money. He says that the management wants to make visitors feel welcome regardless of how much money they spend. It all goes to show what you can do if you have enough money.

Knoebels Groves, in east-central Pennsylvania at Elysburg, is strictly a commercial venture, but you wonder how they can make any money at the prices they charge. A dime still gets the kids a ride on the miniature Ferris wheel or merry-go-round. A ride in a handcar, motorboat, or sports car also is a dime. So is the Fish Pond hanky-pank, although the shooting gallery, basketball, and Shooting Waters are each a quarter. Miniature golf is only half a buck. The big merry-go-round, Sky Slide, and steam train are each 15¢. The big Ferris wheel, roller coaster, Whipper, Helicopter, Flying Cages, and Space Walk are 20¢. You can ride the Satellite, Merry Mixer, RotoJet, or Pioneer Railroad (a 1½-mile woodland excursion) for two bits. The Paratrooper and the Skooters are the most expensive rides—30¢.

Knoebels has gas stoves in the picnic pavilions, and at the big heated swimming pool with its underwater lighting, hair dryers for the ladies are provided in the locker room. The grounds include 250 campsites for tents and trailers at $3 a day (or $18 a week), including an electric hookup and a separate building with unmetered hot and cold showers.

You'd think that a place like that would make it up with stiff prices at a bar or cocktail lounge, but there is no booze of any kind allowed in the park.

Conneaut Lake Park, 40 miles south of Lake Erie and even farther from any sizeable city, is another interesting amusement park cum summer resort. It started on the shores of one of the biggest lakes within the state in 1890 as a chautauqua for the First United Presbyterian Synod. In 1895 it had a School of Pedagogy, but by 1900 it was a full-fledged summer resort with many sizeable hotels, most of which burned down in 1908.

Today, a family of four can stay at the Conneaut Hotel, a quite comfortable old place, for $64 a week. If they stay five days or longer, the kids get free Ride-A-Rama passes (which can also be purchased by day visitors for as little as $2.50), good for unlimited riding on everything but the Jungle Cruise, live ponies, and the steam train. That steam train is a doozy—it's not a miniature or even a replica, but rather an authentic full-scale locomotive operating on a 2-mile trip to nowhere.

Conneaut's leisurely boardwalk has always been almost as popular as the crowded midway, which has 18 games, a fun house, and a Walk-Thru. The Blue Streak roller coaster doesn't streak very fast, but one of its delightful old features is a tight curve directly around the merry-go-round building. That's a combination of sight and sound hard to beat.

PARKS IN PENNSYLVANIA

★★West Mifflin—Kennywood Park. Features pool, beach, miniature golf, pony rides, boating, athletic field, picnic facilities, vaudeville, free acts, fireworks.

★Willow Grove—Willow Grove Park (now called Six Gun Territory). Features fun house, ballroom, picnic facilities, western town, gunfights, stage shows, porpoise show.

★★★Allentown—Dorney Park. Features miniature golf, zoo, theater, racetrack, athletic field, picnic facilities, vaudeville, free acts, fireworks.

★★Conneaut Lake—Conneaut Lake Park. Features fun house,

beach, ballroom, boats, miniature golf, zoo, athletic field, picnic facilities.

★★★★Hershey—Hersheypark. Features fun house, pool, museum, zoo, miniature golf, driving range, athletic field, picnic facilities, vaudeville, free acts.

★★Pittsburgh—West View Park. Features ballroom, miniature golf, pony track, athletic field, picnic facilities.

★Royersford—Lakeview Amusement Park. Features pool, beach, miniature golf, athletic field, picnic facilities.

★★Moosic—Ghost Town in the Glen (formerly Rocky Glen Amusement Park). Features beach, ballroom, zoo, miniature golf, athletic field, picnic facilities, Miss Northeast Pennsylvania Teen-ager contest, National Day celebrations, orchestras, name bands, free acts, fireworks.

★Elysburg—Knoebel's Groves. Features swimming pool, roller rink, ballroom, miniature golf, athletic field, picnic facilities.

★★West Point—West Point Park. Features athletic field, picnic facilities including catering.

★★★★Ligonier—Idlewild Park. Features swimming pool, bathing beach, miniature golf, athletic field, picnic facilities, fireworks.

★Altoona—Lakemont Park. Owned by Blair County. Features Monster Den, pool, roller rink, miniature golf, zoo, boating, athletic field, picnic facilities, name bands, fireworks.

★★Mechanicsburg—Williams Grove Park & Speedway. Features speedway, athletic field, picnic facilities, Great Grangers Picnic Fair & Steam Celebration last week in August and through Labor Day, vaudeville, free acts, fireworks.

★Easton—Bushkill Park. Features fun house, pool, roller rink, theater, athletic field, picnic facilities, free acts.

★Erie—Waldameer Park. Features fun house, ballroom, athletic field, picnic facilities, orchestras, name bands, fireworks.

★★Lewistown—Kishacoquillas Park. Features pool, miniature golf, slot car racing, trailer and tent camping, athletic field, picnic facilities, vaudeville, free acts, fireworks.

★★New Castle—Cascade Park. Features miniature golf, trampolines, boats, picnic facilities, free acts, fireworks.

★★Philadelphia—Kiddie Playland. Features miniature golf, talent search contests.

★★★Hazelton—Angela Park. Features pool, dance pavilion, miniature golf, driving range, athletic field, picnic facilities, orchestras, name bands, vaudeville, free acts, fireworks.

★★Uniontown—Shady Grove Park. Features pool, bathing beach, athletic field, picnic facilities, orchestras, free acts, fireworks.

★★Mechanicsburg—Willow Mill Park. Features miniature golf, athletic field, picnic facilities, orchestras, name bands, free acts, fireworks.

★★Scranton—Nay Aug Amusement Park. Features swimming pool, zoo, picnic facilities.

★★Coraopolis—White Swan Park. Features miniature golf, athletic field, picnic facilities.

★Northampton—Indian Trail Park. Features picnic facilities.

★★Mingoville—Hecla Park. Features pool, roller rink, ballroom, miniature golf, athletic field, picnic facilities, orchestras, name bands, free acts, fireworks.

★★★Johnstown—Fun City Park. Features fun houses, pool, beach, ballroom, Go-Karts, athletic field, picnic facilities.

★★Pine Grove—Twin Grove Park. Features swimming pool, athletic field, picnic facilities, fireworks.

★★★Canadohta Lake Station—Canadohta Lake Park. Features roller rink, ballroom, miniature golf, driving range, stable horses, antique museum, bicycle rentals, beach, boating, fishing, replica passenger steamboat, Miss Sun Queen contest, orchestras, name bands, fireworks.

14: Middle Atlantic States

THE area dominated by the Chesapeake Bay is an entity unto itself. Neither north or south, it is an odd amalgam of cosmopolitan viewpoints, such as those in Washington, D.C., and the most provincial of rural attitudes, such as those on the eastern shore of Maryland. This hodgepodge is reflected in the area's amusement parks, which do not seem able to make up their minds as to whether they are just family picnic groves or the most high-pressure of all amusement park operations.

The biggest concentration of traditional amusement parks in the Middle Atlantic states is at Ocean City, Maryland, where there is a grand total of 41 major rides, 36 kiddie rides, 4 fun houses, a shooting gallery, 8 refreshment stands, a restaurant, 2 Walk-Thrus, and an impressive 45 games.

Those 45 hanky-panks at "the Coney Island of Maryland" include some of the meanest in the industry, but the customers love them. Cottage Grove Amusement Park in Pasadena, Maryland (which passed from the scene in 1972), had a full 30 games backed up with only three major rides. Carr's Beach in Annapolis has only four major rides but has 20 games.

Carr's also has three Walk-Thru attractions. But a Walk-Thru in the tidewater area tends to be more gruesome than in most other parts of the country, almost like a sideshow. Where else would you see an exhibit of giant rats?

Lakeside Amusement Park at Salem, Virginia, is the biggest single amusement park in the area. It has 25 major rides, including a truly great roller coaster. The famous merry-go-round has one of the best band organs in the East. Lakeside also has about two dozen of the most challenging hanky-panks anywhere.

The most interesting park in the area, however, is Marshall Hall Amusement Park, across the Potomac River from Mount Vernon. William Marshall built a house on the grounds in 1690, which still stands today. The Civil War ruined the Marshall family, and the new owners subsequently turned the place into an amusement park in 1876.

Today most of the visitors take the big four-deck excursion boat from downtown Washington to the 500-acre wooded tract. The park is currently operated by Margaret Addison, who became manager in 1958 after the death of her husband, Lorenzo, who had managed the park since 1933. Once each season she takes a ride on each of the 15 major attractions "to check up on the rides and just for the fun of it."

Mrs. Addison has a particularly large following of senior citizens who hold many parties and picnics at the park. Because some of the rides are pretty strenuous, the lost and found department does a brisk business in false teeth and wigs.

Ocean View Amusement Park in Norfolk, Virginia, has the honor of being the site where the world's champion roller coaster riders set their marathon records. As a publicity stunt, Keith James, a nighttime disc jockey, and Sharon Kay Potter boarded the 3,200-foot Sky Rocket when the park opened on Tuesday and rode all day, making every ride until the park closed at night. They did the same Wednesday, Thursday, and Friday. On Saturday they got on at noon and rode straight through until Sunday afternoon. During that 27-hour–45-minute period they made 455 consecutive trips, covering 275 miles.

Only at Carr's Beach in Annapolis, Maryland, can you see 40-pound killer rats imported from the sewers of Paris.

PARKS IN THE MIDDLE ATLANTIC STATES

DELAWARE

★Rehoboth Beach—Seaside Amusements Funland.

MARYLAND

★★Baltimore—Gwynn Oak Park. Features ballroom, miniature golf, athletic field, orchestras, name bands, vaudeville, free acts, fireworks.

★★★Bryans Road—Marshall Hall Amusement Park. Features athletic field, picnic facilities.

★★Ocean City—Trimper Rides and Amusements. Features fun houses, beach.

★★Ocean City—Playland Amusement Park. Features fun house, miniature golf, picnic facilities.

★Ocean City—Ocean City Amusement Pier. Features fun house.

★★Ocean City—Jolly Roger Park. Features miniature golf, driving range, racetrack.

★★★Chesapeake Beach—Chesapeake Beach Park. Features fun house, pool, beach, ballroom, marina, rowboats, charter boats, athletic field, picnic facilities, orchestras, vaudeville, free acts.

★★Newburgh—Aqua-Land Park. Features ballroom, beach, marina, zoo, Storyville, bingo, athletic field, picnic facilities, orchestras, name bands, free acts, fireworks.

★★★Annapolis—Carr's Beach. Features cocktail lounge, aquacade pavilion, beach, boat rides, athletic field, picnic facilities, midget auto races, bathing beauty contests, orchestras, name bands, free acts, fireworks.

★Baltimore—Bay Shore Park. Features beach, ballroom, picnic facilities, orchestras.

VIRGINIA

★★★Salem—Lakeside Amusement Park. Features ballroom, swimming pool, miniature golf, picnic facilities, orchestras, name bands, free acts, fireworks.

★★Norfolk—Ocean View Amusement Park. Features fun house, ballroom, miniature golf, beach, zoo, picnic facilities, orchestras, free acts, fireworks.

★★Buckroe Beach—Buckroe Beach Amusement Park. Features fun house, beach, ballroom, miniature golf, picnic facilities, orchestras.

★Virginia Beach—Seaside Amusement Park. Features beach, ballroom, picnic facilities, orchestras, free acts, fireworks.

★★Colonial Beach—Reno Park. Features swimming pool, beach, ballroom, orchestras, name bands, free acts, fireworks.

15: The South

Operators of traditional amusement parks in the South have been somewhat intimidated by the new theme parks growing up around them, which include some of the biggest operations in the industry, such as Opryland and Six Flags Over Georgia (see Chapter 21). But that's no excuse for letting a good old park go to seed. Parks across the rest of the country are still doing all right because they operate on the premise that they have more to offer than a theme park; but the South just doesn't seem to have its heart in the business anymore. There are plenty of parks in the South—some three dozen of them—but most are pitifully shabby. Instead of growing, which plenty of parks in the United States are doing, the average Southern park is getting smaller all the time. For example, when a ride breaks down, it's simply shuttered for good. A terrible loss.

The only really great park in the entire South is Beech Bend Park, Bowling Green, Kentucky. And the only reason Beech Bend is considered great is because it has some three dozen major rides —not because of the way they are maintained. The roller coaster cars, in particular, have seen better days.

Nashville's Opryland greets its visitors with the likes of Yancy Banjo.

The General, located at Six Flags Over Georgia, is a 3/4 scale replica of the famous original.

Children visiting Dogpatch, U.S.A., Arkansas, can become part of a mule train.

You can find a relatively new Trabant ride once in a while, but the South is mostly pony ride territory. But what else can you expect in an area where the penny arcades feature horoscope machines and Cupid's Post Office, where a patron can buy himself a love letter? Most of the new equipment is some type of bumper car. The South is very big on the Dodgem, and even some of the smaller parks have big Skooter layouts. Most of the newer models are built in Italy at the Spaggiari factory, which is now the world's largest supplier of bumper cars. Owners of Spaggiari bumper cars noted in the South include Crystal Beach in Elizabethtown, North Carolina; Lake Winnepesaukah in Rossville, Georgia; Burns Park Funland in North Little Rock, Arkansas; and Beech Bend Park.

Aside from a better than average bumper car layout, Crystal Beach has only eight other rides, but there are also some 200 hanky-panks in operation. There's also a motel on the premises, although it's nothing to brag about.

Neither is the 365-room hotel at Callaway Gardens, Pine Mountain, Georgia, nor the 155 cottages. The little 6-ride amusement park has eight Walk-Thrus, but this is basically a summer resort with a 63-hole golf course (too easy), fishing lake, and hunting preserve.

Lake Spivey Park, Jonesboro, Georgia, isn't so bad, thanks more to its 2-mile beach than to the rides and concessions. On Saturdays and Sundays there's a pretty good water ski show called the Ski Follies, and there's a free ski school as well. The management is also making an attempt to cash in on the theme park boom with the construction of Fort Spivey.

Pioneerland attractions at the Lake Winnepesaukah Amusement Parks (Chattanooga, Tennessee and Rossville, Georgia) represent similar attempts, but they seem halfhearted. Considering that these parks are owned by women—Evelyn Dixon White, president, Adrienne White Rhodes, secretary, and Charlyn White Harless, vice-president, gift buyer and game superintendant—they ought to have better housekeeping. Never mind the gift buyer— what Winnepesaukah needs is a more active paint buyer.

Doe River Gorge Playland, Hampton, Tennessee, has a 6-mile

scenic railway going for it, but it is down to seven major rides, a couple of Walk-Thrus, a dinky penny arcade, and half a dozen or so games. Fortunately, the scenery is magnificent.

PARKS IN THE SOUTH

NORTH CAROLINA

★★Elizabethtown—Crystal Beach. Features fun house, ballroom, beach, marina, sight-seeing boat, miniature golf, motel, campground, picnic facilities, orchestras, name bands.

★★Hillsborough—Daniel Boone Railroad Park. Features ice rink, antique car museum, wax museum, theater, hotel, campground.

★White Lake—Goldston's Beach. Features picnic facilities.

★Carolina Beach—Sea Shore Amusement Park.

★White Lake—Crystal Beach. Features fishing pier, boat rental.

★★Asheville—Asheville Recreation Park. Features fun house, golf driving range, swimming pool, zoo, picnic facilities, fireworks.

★★Southport—Yaupon Amusement Park. Features miniature golf, picnic facilities.

★Atlantic Beach—Anchor Green Amusement Park. Features miniature golf, picnic facilities.

SOUTH CAROLINA

★★Myrtle Beach—Myrtle Beach Pavilion & Amusement Park. Features fun house, beach, ballroom, miniature golf courses, picnic facilities, orchestras, name bands, free acts, fireworks.

★Folly Beach—Folly Beach Amusement Park. Features dance halls, cocktail lounge, miniature golf, beach, picnic facilities, orchestras, name bands, fireworks.

★Myrtle Beach—Grand Strand Amusement Park. Features beach.

★Myrtle Beach—Astro Needle Park.

★North Myrtle Beach—Ocean Drive Amusement Park.

★North Myrtle Beach—North Myrtle Beach Amusement Park.

★North Myrtle Beach—Crescent Beach Pavilion.

GEORGIA

★Rossville—Lake Winnepesaukah. Features paddle boats, outdoor theater, miniature golf, picnic facilities, Birthday Cake House, Pioneerland, free acts, fireworks.

★★★Jonesboro—Lake Spivey Park. Features miniature golf, Fort Spivey, beach, picnic facilities, free waterskiing show, name bands.

★★Pine Mountain—Callaway Gardens. Features ballroom, swimming pool, beach, tennis courts, theater, athletic field, picnic facilities, regulation golf course, hunting preserve, fishing lake, orchestras, free acts, fireworks, motel, cottages.

★St. Simons Island—Neptune Park Casino. Features theater, pool, beach, roller rink, bowling, miniature golf, athletic field, picnic facilities, fireworks.

KENTUCKY

★★★★Bowling Green—Beech Bend Park. Features pool, roller rink, racetrack, miniature golf, Go-Karts, trampolines, zoo, picnic facilities, stock car and drag races, horse stables, fishing, camping, name bands, free acts, fireworks.

★★Paducah—Noble Park Funland. Features fun house, swimming pool, athletic field, picnic facilities, free acts, fireworks.

WEST VIRGINIA

★★Huntington—Camden Park. Features roller rink, miniature golf, zoo, horse show grounds, picnic facilities, vaudeville, free acts, fireworks.

TENNESSEE

★Chattanooga—Lake Winnepesaukah. Features miniature golf, outdoor theater, canoeing, Birthday Cake House, picnic facilities, Pioneerland, free acts, fireworks.

★Memphis—Fairgrounds Amusement Park. City owned. Features athletic field, picnic facilities, fireworks.

★Knoxville—Chilhowee Park. Features fun house, roller rink, ballroom, zoo, miniature golf, outdoor theater, athletic field, picnic facilities, city-owned horse show ring, stables, wrestling, name bands, free acts, fireworks.

★★Memphis—Lakeland Amusement Park. Features swimming pool, Go-Karts, auto racetrack, trailer park, campgrounds, picnic facilities.

★★★Hampton—Doe River Gorge Playland. Features scenic train ride, beach, miniature golf, driving range, zoo, free campgrounds, athletic field, picnic facilities, vaudeville, free acts, fireworks.

★★Nashville—Fair Amusement Park. Features fun house, pool, miniature golf, picnic facilities, fireworks.

★★Chattanooga—Warner Park. City owned. Features pool, beach, miniature golf, bird collection, athletic field, field house, picnic facilities, fireworks.

ALABAMA

★Birmingham—Fair Park Kiddieland. Owned by Alabama State Fair Authority. Features fun house, archery range, racetrack, athletic field, picnic facilities.

★Decatur—Funland Park. Features roller rink, miniature golf, billiards, picnic facilities.

MISSISSIPPI

Biloxi—Biloxi-Gulfport Amusement Park. Features beach, picnic facilities, free acts, fireworks.

ARKANSAS

★Little Rock—War Memorial Park. Features fun house, swimming pool, miniature golf, city zoo, archery, athletic field, ball park, football stadium, picnic facilities, fireworks.

★★North Little Rock—Burns Park Funland. Features miniature golf, athletic field, picnic facilities, free acts, fireworks.

★★Jonesboro—Funland Park. Features roller rink, boating, pitch and putt golf course, water sports, picnic facilities, orchestras, free acts, fireworks.

16: Gulf States

THE areas bordering the Gulf of Mexico have long been dedicated to pleasure, and to the attracting of tourists. Amusement parks have existed there ever since the invention of the steam-powered merry-go-round.

Business is brisk for traditional amusement parks all over Florida, despite competition from a couple of dozen theme parks scattered throughout the state. The only major park that couldn't make the grade was Wonderland, at Indian River City, but that is practically in the backyard of the cluster of theme parks growing up around Disney World at Orlando. Even the installation of such thematic attractions as a marine show, a jungle trail, and stage-coach rides with simulated Wild West gun battles couldn't keep Florida's Wonderland alive.

The Old West Kiddie Park in North Miami Beach is a kiddie park in name only. When the kiddie business petered out, the park added more major rides as well as a *quite* adult penny arcade.

The Jacksonville area has three amusement parks, all in the

Big Tex annually welcomes visitors
to the Texas State Fair.

State Fair Park in Dallas has one of the biggest fun houses in the United States.

Fort Worth's Forest Park operates three miniature railroads.

traditional mold. Best of the three is Jacksonville Beach Board-walk, with a dozen major rides, 10 kiddie rides, 2 shooting galleries, a well-equipped penny arcade, and 15 hanky-panks, along with half a dozen refreshment stands and 5 complete restaurants. The noise from the midway doesn't seem to bother the fish—good catches are constantly made from the park's fishing pier that juts out into the Atlantic Ocean.

On the Gulf side of the state, in Panama City, is another whole complex of amusement parks. One of them, Petticoat Junction, is technically a theme park because it was built on the television show's success. The theme is now largely ignored, and the park has most of the rides and concessions found in any traditional park. In fact, Petticoat Junction has the best roller coaster in the state—the super-fast Tornado.

Panama City's Playland is the biggest traditional park in the state, with 18 major rides, a dozen kiddie rides, and 10 games. Down the road, Miracle Strip Amusement Park doesn't have quite as many rides, but it does have three fun houses, three Walk-Thrus, more refreshment stands, a Jungle Land, bathing beach, scenic tower, and a shooting gallery that Playland lacks. Unfortunately, Miracle Strip is operated as a blatant tourist trap.

To find one of the really great amusement parks on the Gulf, go to Louisiana and visit Pontchartrain Beach in New Orleans. The older rides and attractions aren't aging very gracefully, but there is a porpoise show now and a miniature golf course cornily called Around the World in 18 Holes. Although Pontchartrain is not so big—it has only 16 major rides—it has always maintained a true amusement park atmosphere in the great tradition. Some of the gravel-voiced old guys have worked the hanky-panks on the midway for half a century.

In Texas, State Fair Park in Dallas has almost three times as many major rides as the next largest amusement park in the state. It also has Big Tex, the 55-foot cowboy statue serving as a symbol of the spirit and scope of the nation's biggest state fair held on the grounds every year.

Tex's steel skeleton was built in 1949 for the Christmas holiday in Kerens, Texas. After using the huge Santa Claus for two years, the Kerens Chamber of Commerce sold him to the fair, where he was promptly converted into a cowboy. Today he is dressed in real blue jeans (size 276), a size 90 plaid shirt, size 70 boots, and a 75-gallon hat. His head is 8 feet high, and his smile is a yard wide. He is wired for sound, and when Big Tex talks, you listen.

In keeping with the Texas propensity for having everything bigger (though not necessarily better), State Fair Park has one of the biggest fun houses in America. Two stories high and maybe half a block deep, it is modeled after the famous Hofbrau House in Zurich, Switzerland. In all, the midway has some 300 amusement devices and activities.

PARKS IN THE GULF STATES

FLORIDA

★★Panama City—Playland Amusement Park. Features fun house, picnic facilities, free acts, fireworks.

★Panama City—Miracle Strip Amusement Park. Features fun houses, scenic tower, beach, miniature golf, Jungleland, fireworks.

★★★Jacksonville Beach—Jacksonville Beach Boardwalk. Owned by Jacksonville Beach Chamber of Commerce. Features theater, miniature golf, beach, fishing pier, picnic facilities, orchestras, fireworks.

★★Jacksonville Beach—Griffen Amusement Park. Features picnic facilities, fireworks, beauty contests, water shows, concerts, spring band festival.

★North Miami Beach—Old West Kiddie Park.

★★Jacksonville—Riverview Amusement Park. Features fun house, roller rink, ballroom, picnic facilities, orchestras.

★Daytona Beach—Forest Amusement Park. Features beach.

★★Miami—P.B.A. Amusement Park. Owned by the Miami Police Benevolent Association. Features pony rides, barbecue pit area, ballroom, athletic field, picnic facilities, orchestras, fireworks.

LOUISIANA

★★★★New Orleans—Pontchartrain Beach. Features miniature golf, beach, picnic facilities, some of the best fireworks in the South.

★★Baton Rouge—Fun Fair Park. Features theater, picnic facilities.

★Alexandria—City Park Funland. Features pool, roller rink, miniature golf, zoo, Skee Ball pavilion, athletic field, picnic facilities, free acts.

★★Watson—Thunderbird Amusement Park. Features swimming pool, beach, paddle boats, miniature golf, zoo, picnic facilities, name bands, free acts, fireworks.

★★New Orleans—Kiddieland Audubon Park. Features pony rides, miniature train, stable horses, zoo, bicycle rentals, golf course, athletic field, picnic facilities, orchestras, name bands, vaudeville, free acts.

★New Orleans—Park Amusements, Inc. Features miniature golf, driving range, picnic facilities.

TEXAS

★★★★Dallas—State Fair Amusement Park. Owned by State Fair of Texas. Features roller rink, ice rink, wax museum, picnic facilities. Cotton Bowl Stadium, Coliseum, and Music Hall are also on the grounds.

★★Amarillo—Wonderland Amusement Center. Features miniature golf, picnic facilities.

★★★San Antonio—Playland Park. Features fun house, miniature golf, picnic facilities, free acts, fireworks.

★★El Paso—Western Playland, Ascarate Park. Features Mirror Maze, picnic facilities, name bands, free acts, fireworks.

★★Dallas—Sandy Lake Amusement Park. Features swimming pool, kids' barnyard, miniature golf, picnic facilities, free acts, fireworks.

★★Wichita Falls—Funland Amusement Park. Features miniature golf, picnic facilities.

★★★Galveston—Kiddieland Amusement Park. Features fun house, beach, roller rink, miniature golf, picnic facilities.

★★Lubbock—MacKenzie Park Playground. Features pool, picnic facilities.

★San Angelo—Neff's Amusement Park. Features free acts.

★★Texarkana—Happytime, U.S.A. Features miniature golf.

★Abilene—Nelson Park. Features swimming pool, beach, roller rink, zoo, miniature golf, miniature boat rides, picnic facilities, fireworks.

★★★Dallas—Vickery Amusement Park. Features pool, beach, ponies, ballroom, miniature golf, archery range, athletic field, picnic facilities, orchestras, name bands, fireworks.

17

17: The Midwest

THE best amusement park in the United States is Cedar Point, in Sandusky, Ohio. All of the old rides have been kept in tiptop condition—the Blue Streak roller coaster probably has none of the original nuts, bolts, or boards still left in it. New rides and features are added every year. No new ride is invented anywhere in the world without Cedar Point checking it out to see if it might make a good addition.

Cedar Point's 39 major rides include the biggest Ferris wheel in North America. With a total of over 200 rides and attractions, the park has more ride capacity than any other place in the world —close to 100,000 rides per hour. The park has a 300-foot Space Tower, two separate Sky Rides, two miniature trains (and they're not all that miniature, either), three paddle-wheel riverboats, four roller coasters (five, if you count the Log Flume ride), and three merry-go-rounds. The Frontier Town is the most complete theme-park-within-an-amusement-park in the country. There are 3 Walk-Thrus, 2 penny arcades, 2 shooting galleries, and 3 theaters, plus 34 refreshment stands and 13 restaurants—and the food is good.

Everything at Cedar Point is repainted and refurbished every spring, from the 200-slip marina on the bay side of the peninsula to the 1,000-room Breakers Hotel on the Lake Erie side of the point. A corps of shorts-uniformed college and high school girls keep the grounds cleaned up. The crowds cooperate, too; so there's very little litter. The customers seem to appreciate the way Cedar Point tries its best to do everything possible to give them a good time—all on a one-price policy.

Cedar Point's dedication to excellence has paid off. The operation grosses some $25 million a year.

But it wasn't always so successful. Its spotty 100-year history reached a crisis in the 1940s and early 1950s, when it looked as if its days were numbered. An investment group, headed by Emile Legros and George Roose, acquired the property in 1957 and, in desperation to protect their investment, took over active management themselves in 1959. It took them ten years to clean up the park and build it to a $12.5 million per year business. In an intensive program of improvements, highlighted by the construction of the Giant Wheel in 1972, they doubled that figure within the next five years.

The year 1968 was shake-up year at Cedar Point. Several former officials, including Earl Gascoigne, Gaspar Lococo, and Dale Van Voorhis, broke away and bought the old Geauga Lake Amusement Park 20 miles east of Cleveland. They went public to raise working capital and have been putting approximately $1 million a year into improvements ever since. Geauga Lake Park had had a $500,000 fire in the 1950s, so there was plenty to improve.

The heart of the old park was one of the most dismal penny arcades in America, but the reborn Geauga Lake now has 30 major rides and numerous other attractions, including the only monorail and the largest kiddieland in the Midwest. The new owners are approaching the one-price plan somewhat cautiously— they still offer an alternative pay-by-the ride policy.

The one-price policy was pioneered in southern Ohio by Howard Berni and Bill Barr when they took over LeSourdsville Lake Amusement Park, between Cincinnati and Dayton, in the 1960s. They have added new attractions every season, including a

Cincinnati's Coney Island was always the most up-to-date amusement park in the country, due to renovations after numerous floods.

Aerial view of LeSourdesville Lake. Pinocchio Land is at the left

Thanks to cooperative patrons, Cedar Point in Sandusky, Ohio, is practically litter-free.

Geauga Lake circa 1927. Gawkers paid 10¢ just to get in to watch.

The mall at LeSourdesville Lake is curved in a semicircle around the lake, providing easy access to the wide variety of rides and games.

The famous "Albert," restored in 1959, now is owned and operated by Cedar Point Park, Sandusky, Ohio.

Sky Ride 60 feet over the lake, an air-conditioned penny arcade, and a new Tombstone Territory with two dozen Old West storefront displays around the Dry Gulch Saloon (complete with dancing girls). Latest additions are the Calypso and Sombrero rides and the Indy 500.

LeSourdsville's Kiddie Kingdom, called Pinocchio Land in the old days, is now unique in that it has a lot of giant plastic animals for the kids to climb around on. The old Cyclone roller coaster, renamed the Space Rocket, still has the same tracks, but all of the cars are new.

The best roller coaster in Ohio, however, is still the Jack Rabbit at Idora, Youngstown's old trolley park. It has the most complex system of track interweaves of any roller coaster still in existence. Idora Park also has the biggest ballroom between New York and Chicago, with over 22,000 square feet of space capable of accommodating 5,000 dancers.

Just as many traditional amusement parks now include small theme parks, some theme parks have added small traditional amusement parks. Kings Island Park, a theme park at Kings Mills, contains an amusement park mostly comprised of the remnants of Cincinnati's well-remembered Coney Island. There are ten rides, four games, a couple of refreshment stands—all excellently operated. But the flavor of the hot dogs is not the same, and everything is a little too cute.

In the river just below Detroit and huddled against the Canadian shore is one of the all-time greats—Bob Lo Island Amusement Park. What can you say about a once magnificent park that's dying? It gets a 4-star rating strictly out of sentiment.

In contrast to wonderful old Bob Lo, the new Indiana Beach Amusement Park, near Monticello, Indiana, is booming spectacularly. It already has 18 major rides, with more being added each year. The Galaxie roller coaster is built on its own pier next to the dock where passengers board the *Shafer Queen*, a 250-passenger sight-seeing diesel riverboat with a stern paddle wheel, two decks, and typical Mississippi high-rise smokestacks. Indiana Beach is in one of the best locations in the country, halfway between Indianapolis and Chicago. A motel, cottages, and a 150-acre campsite accommodate overnight visitors.

What can be said about Illinois, except that Riverview Park used to be there? The best the state now has to offer is the commercial Playland Amusement Park in Willow Springs. Playland, however, is growing every year. Maybe it really is better than it seems to someone who can't help comparing it to Riverview.

PARKS IN THE MIDWEST

OHIO

★★★★Sandusky—Cedar Point. Features fun house, beach, marina, miniature golf, theaters, Safariland, Sealand, Frontier Trail, trailer park, hotel, ferry boats, picnic facilities.

★★★★Aurora—Geauga Lake Park. Features fun house, ballroom, miniature golf, picnic facilities.

★★★Chippewa Lake—Chippewa Lake Amusement Park. Features fun house, swimming pool, beach, ballroom, miniature golf, sheltered outdoor theater, athletic field, picnic facilities, orchestras, name bands, free acts, fireworks.

★★Middletown—LeSourdsville Lake. Features fun house, swimming pool, beach, ballroom, miniature golf, western town, horses, ponies, animals, athletic field, picnic facilities, orchestras, free acts, fireworks.

★★★Youngstown—Idora Amusement Park. Features ballroom, miniature golf, athletic field, picnic facilities, orchestras, name bands, fireworks.

★★Akron—Playland Park, Inc. Features German band organ, ponies, miniature golf, picnic facilities, orchestras, fireworks.

★★Russells Point—Indian Lake Playland Park. Features dark ride, fun house, ballroom, miniature golf, marina, picnic facilities.

★Buckeye Lake—Buckeye Lake Park. Features fun house, swimming pool, beach, roller rink, ballrooms, miniature golf, bowling, nightclub, speedboats, yachting, excursion boat, athletic field, picnic facilities, orchestras, name bands, fireworks, water shows.

★★Powell—Gooding's Zoo & Amusement Park. Features zoo, miniature golf, athletic field, ballroom, picnic facilities.

★★Kings Mills (Cincinnati)—Coney Island. One of five theme parks that comprise the Kings Island complex (others: Rivertown, Oktoberfest, International Street, and The Happy Land of Hanna-Barbera). Features motel, campground with pool, regulation and championship golf courses, theater, emporium, daily musical revues, vaudeville, barbershop quartets, dixieland bands, 330-foot replica of the Eiffel Tower.

★★Canton—Meyers Lake Park. Features fun house, miniature golf, athletic field, picnic facilities, orchestras, name bands, fireworks.

★Cincinnati—Cincinnati Concession Company. Features fun house, pool, miniature golf, ballroom, boats, athletic field, orchestras, name bands, vaudeville, free acts, fireworks.

★★Cincinnati—Lunken Airport Playfield Kiddie-Land. Features picnic facilities.

★Bascom—Meadowbrook Park. Features swimming pools, ballroom, miniature golf, theater, camping, athletic field, picnic facilities, free acts.

★Cincinnati—Cincinnati Zoo. Features ballroom, picnic facilities, orchestras, name bands.

★★Geneva-On-The-Lake—Pera's Amusement Park. Features fun house, beach, swimming pool, ballroom, nightclub, hotels, motel, cottages, picnic facilities, orchestras, name bands.

★★★Garrettsville—Nelson Ledge Amusement Park. Features driving range, zoo, campgrounds, hiking trails, caves, caverns, swimming, boating, fishing, athletic field, picnic facilities, auctions every Sunday, fireworks. Rides are being phased out.

MICHIGAN

★★★★Detroit—Bob-Lo Island Amusement Park (actually in Ontario, Canada). Features fun houses, miniature golf, athletic field, picnic facilities, roller rink, ballroom, marina, pony rides, excursion boats, children's puppet theater, zoo, train ride.

★★★Detroit—Edgewater Park. Features fun houses, miniature golf, athletic field, picnic facilities, free acts, name bands, vaudeville.

★Haslett—Lake Lansing Park. Features miniature golf, boat slip, athletic field, picnic facilities, free acts, fireworks.

★★Richmond—King Animaland Park. Features fun house, athletic field, picnic facilities, free circus shows daily.

★★LaSalle—Kress Toledo Beach. Features fun house, ballroom, kiddie playground, beach, camping facilities, athletic field, picnic facilities.

★★Sterling Heights—Utica Amusement Park. Features ballroom, miniature golf, athletic field, picnic facilities, orchestras, free acts, fireworks.

★★Bay City—Tony's Amusement Park. Features roller rink, outdoor ballroom, miniature golf, athletic field, picnic facilities, name bands.

INDIANA

★★Monticello—Indiana Beach. Features ballroom, beach, marina, sight-seeing boats, miniature golf, driving range, hotel, cottages, picnic facilities, orchestras, name bands, free acts, fireworks.

★★★Chesterton—Enchanted Forest Amusement Park. Features fun house, children's zoo, 150 tame deer, picnic facilities, free acts.

★★North Webster—Adventureland. Features miniature golf courses, picnic facilities.

★★Angola—Buck Lake Ranch. Features ballroom, outdoor theater, early American museum, boating, trout fishing, athletic field, picnic facilities, vaudeville, wrestling, free acts, fireworks.

★Evansville—Mesker Park.

★★Schereville—Sauzer's Kiddieland Amusement Park. Features fireworks.

★★Lafayette—Columbian Park. Features pony rides, pool, beach, ballroom, outdoor theater, miniature golf, zoo, athletic field, picnic facilities, fireworks.

★★Marion—Matter Park Kiddieland. Features swimming pool, athletic field, picnic facilities, vaudeville, free acts, fireworks.

★Merrillville—Merriland Amusement Park. Features 12-lane slide, athletic field, picnic facilities.

ILLINOIS

★★★Addison—Adventureland. Features fun house, picnic facilities, free acts.

★★Dundee—Santa's Village. Features ice rink, Santa's House, trained animals, picnic facilities.

★★★Willow Springs—Playland Amusement Park. Features fun house, racetrack, picnic facilities.

★★Chicago—Funtown Amusement Park. Features miniature golf, driving range, picnic facilities, free acts, fireworks.

★★Melrose Park—Kiddieland. Features fire engines.

★★Lyons—Fairyland Park. Features zoo, picnic facilities.

★★Chicago—Hollywood Kiddieland. Features miniature golf, driving range.

★Rockford—Sherwood Park. Features ballroom, miniature golf, zoo, athletic field, picnic facilities, orchestras, name bands, vaudeville, free acts.

★Decatur—Joyland. Features miniature golf.

★Richton Park—Hilltop Amusement Park. Features Go-Karts, picnic facilities.

★Lemont—Acorn Ridge Park. Features ballroom, snowmobile rentals, picnic facilities.

★★Danville—Douglas Park. Features athletic field, picnic facilities, free acts.

★★Ingleside—Holiday Park. Features miniature golf, beach, ski slopes, athletic field, picnic facilities, orchestras, fireworks.

★Galesburg—Galesburg Amusement Park.

★★East Moline—Starlite Amusement Park. Features racetrack, picnic facilities.

★★Paris—Twin Lakes Park. Features beach, miniature golf, camping, athletic field, picnic facilities, free acts, fireworks.

★★Lake Zurich—Nestlerest Park. Features ballroom, beach, athletic field, picnic facilities, orchestras, vaudeville.

★Waukegan—K-ze-K Amusement Park. Features Go-Karts, baseball batting cages.

WISCONSIN

★★★Muskego—Dandilion Park. Features beach, ballroom, zoo, kiddie zoo, theater, puppet theater, athletic field, picnic facilities, orchestras, name bands, free acts, fireworks.

★Milwaukee—Capitol Court (also known as Funtown).

★★Lake Delton—Familyland. Features fun house, picnic facilities.

★★Green Bay—Beach Bay Amusement Park. Features old-time popcorn wagon, wildlife sanctuary, athletic field, picnic facilities, orchestras, name bands, fireworks.

MINNESOTA

★Excelsior—Excelsior Amusement Park. Features roller rink, ballroom, miniature golf, marina.

★★St. Paul—Como Park. Features swimming pool, ice rink, miniature golf, regulation golf course, zoo, conservatory, fire engine and train exhibit, athletic field, picnic facilities.

MISSOURI

★★Kansas City—Fairyland Park. Features fun house, swimming pool, theater, athletic field, picnic facilities, orchestras, name bands, fireworks.

★St. Louis—Chain-of-Rocks Fun Fair Park. Features fun house, pool, ballroom, miniature golf, athletic field, picnic facilities, orchestras, free acts, fireworks.

★★★Kansas City—Worlds of Fun. Features porpoise show, petting zoo, theaters, steam train, picnic facilities, name bands for special occasions, free acts, fireworks.

★★★Springfield—Doling Amusement Park. Features fun houses, roller rink, ballroom, Skee Ball pavilion, boating, athletic field, picnic facilities, fireworks, free acts.

★St. Louis—Holiday Hill. Features fun house, pool, miniature golf, standard golf course, archery, picnic facilities.

★★Lake Ozark—Lake of the Ozarks Amusement Park. Features swimming pool, campground, picnic facilities.

★★St. Joseph—Lake Contrary Amusement Park. Features fun house, ballroom, athletic field, picnic facilities, free acts, fireworks.

★★Blue Spring—Homestead Farm. Features picnic facilities.

18: Plains States

Riverview Park lives! But it's in Des Moines, Iowa, and bears the same relation to Chicago's Riverview as Cincinnati's Coney Island bears to the real Coney Island in New York. The names were just swiped.

The Iowa Riverview has an odd history. After a visit to Chicago, where they saw how Bill Schmidt was raking in the money, W. E. Kooker and Abe Frankle went home to start a wacky corporation in which the 30 stockholders were mainly the concessionaires for the proposed park. When the park opened in 1915, the majority of the rides and games were not owned by the Riverview Amusement Corporation but by individuals—the most prominent being Eli Bookey—who had formed their own little companies. Through the years the corporation bought out these companies by issuing stock as payment, and today all the stock is held by the Kooker and Bookey families. Bart Kooker, a grandson, now runs the park. Old W. E. Kooker, alive and well at 92 years of age in the winter of 1972, said he would organize Riverview the same way again if he had it all to do over.

His original gate admission was a nickel, and the average patron's expenditure was 42¢. Even today the penny arcade still has
machines that operate for a penny, and the highest priced ride is
the 40¢ roller coaster. Many rides are 20¢. On Wednesday after-
noons, Kid's Day, the rides are from 7¢ to 21¢.

Kooker and Frankle tried to use every good idea Bill Schmidt
ever had. When he got a Scrambler, they got one. They built a
Chutes because the Chicago Chutes was the most popular ride in
the Midwest. When they built their House of Mirth they hired
Zarro Amusements, which had built the fun house in Chicago,
and got an exact duplicate. Their roller coaster, though, is unique
—all eight of its dips go clear to the ground. Built in 1920, it is still
a darned good roller coaster, with a tunnel at the beginning and a
full 1½-mile track.

Arnolds Park, Iowa, has become somewhat of an amusement
center with two separate parks. Between them, they now have 23
major rides, 19 kiddie rides, a fun house, 3 Walk-Thrus, 11 games,
10 refreshment stands, and 3 restaurants. Both also have penny
arcades, shooting galleries, beaches, and a choice between several
motels and cottages.

The best amusement park in the Plains states is the somewhat
small but uniformly excellent Peony Park in Omaha, Nebraska.
Peony Park has only ten major rides, but they include a new
2,000-foot Galaxy roller coaster, a 75-foot Skydiver as well as a
conventional Ferris wheel, an Octopus, and a Paratrooper. The
air-conditioned arcade building has 50 machines, including 10
Skee Ball automatics. Except for some of the kiddie rides that
date back to 1958, there's no ride in the park more than 12 years
old.

The Royal Terrace Ballroom operates the year around at
Peony Park. Its gardens are magnificent, although no peonies
were planted because those flowers last for such a short time. The
swimming pool is one of the largest in the country, and there's
picnicking every day, rain or shine. The Omaha Symphony Pop
Concerts, held in the open air all summer, rival anything west of
Chicago.

Perhaps the best miniature train in the Plains states is operated by Joyland Park in Wichita.

Only one of the colorful attractions at Omaha's Peony Park.

Peony Park has started to feel out the one-price policy trend. The first season they tried it—in 1972—business doubled.

The two largest parks in the Plains states are both in Oklahoma: Bell's Amusement Park in Tulsa and Springlake Amusement Park in Oklahoma City. Both are pretty good parks, but Bell's takes the edge because of the yearly improvements.

Bell's roller coaster, Zingo, is not only one of the world's largest wooden coasters but also one of the newest—built by the Philadelphia Toboggan Company in 1968. Robert Kiwanis Bell was a part-time builder of amusement park rides while working for the post office, and he personally built five of the first six rides for his own park, which opened in 1951. He continued to work the night shift at the post office for five years, while operating the park in the early evening. Finally when the park was a prosperous concern, Bell started devoting his full time to it, traveling all over the country to add new rides every season. In 1972 he shopped Europe for a Himalaya, and he installed another new ride in 1973, the huge dark ride designed by Bill Tracy of New Jersey, called Phantasmagoria. The Skee Ball now has 40 alleys, and a third 18-hole miniature golf layout, now under construction, will make a 54-hole golf course. What makes Bell's Park big is not acreage, but its number of attractions, including 16 major rides, all packed into 11 acres.

Springlake has the biggest covered picnic pavilion in the state and one of the biggest penny arcades anywhere. The amphitheater puts on some pretty good shows, and the park has a rarity in the industry—a cafeteria. Springlake's patrons have the option of a pay gate or a one-price policy ticket.

The best miniature train in this whole Plains territory is the one at Joyland Amusement Park in Wichita, Kansas. The brass fittings on the locomotive are kept so highly polished that the kids tell each other that they are made of gold. Many old-timers come just to sit and watch it, although not so many anymore since the park established a minimum-purchase gate. Wags in the industry kiddingly say that Joyland's owner, Stan Nelson, was elected president of the International Association of Amusement Parks in

1972 so that the board of directors could get free rides on his miniature railroad.

PARKS IN THE PLAINS STATES

IOWA

★Des Moines—Riverview Park. Features ballroom, miniature golf, zoo, speedboat rides, picnic facilities, fireworks.

★Arnolds Park—Benit Amusement Park. Features nightclub, roller rink, beach, miniature golf, cottages, picnic facilities, excursion boats, fireworks.

★★Arnolds Park—Arnolds Park Amusement Enterprises, Inc. Features fun house, ballroom, beach, speedboats, cruisers, marina, teen canteen, motel, athletic field, picnic facilities, orchestras, name bands, teen acts, free acts, fireworks, beauty contests.

★★Fort Dodge—Jolly Giant Fun Park. Features miniature golf, driving range, picnic facilities, free acts, fireworks.

★★Clear Lake—Smokey's Amusement Park. Features miniature golf, batting range, picnic facilities.

★Burlington—Burlington Amusement Center. Features picnic facilities.

NEBRASKA

★★★★Omaha—Peony Park. Features beach, indoor and outdoor ballrooms, banquet and picnic catering, miniature golf, athletic field, picnic facilities, orchestras, name bands, fireworks.

KANSAS

★★★Wichita—Joyland Amusement Park. Features pool, roller

rink, miniature golf, athletic field, picnic facilities, Frontier Town theme operation, free acts, fireworks.

★★Topeka—Joyland Park. Features miniature golf, picnic facilities, free acts.

★Salina—Playland Park. Features miniature golf, Go-Karts.

★★Hutchinson—Carey's Park. Features beach, swimming pool, athletic field, picnic facilities.

OKLAHOMA

★★★Oklahoma City—Springlake Amusement Park. Features fun house, Mirror Maze, miniature golf, amphitheater, picnic facilities, orchestras, name bands, fireworks.

★★★Tulsa—Bell's Amusement Park. Features miniature golf, athletic field, picnic facilities.

★Jenks—Indian Nations Park. Features swimming pool, beach, ballroom, zoo, picnic facilities, fireworks.

★★★Cache—Eagle Park. Features roller rink, miniature golf, historical displays, rodeo arena, stable horses, picnic facilities, free acts, fireworks.

★★Oklahoma City—Lincoln Park. Features picnic facilities.

★★Oklahoma City—Oklahoma City Zoo. City owned. Features tram rides, zoo, major exhibits.

19:   Western States

There's a lot more going on in the western states than Disneyland. Two parks that rank with the best in the world are out West—Elitch's Gardens in Colorado and Lagoon Amusement Park in Utah.

What started out in 1891 as a zoological garden in an old Denver apple orchard, with a vaudeville pavilion as a cultural lure, has developed into Elitch's Gardens. The park is many things to many people. To visitors from all over the world, it is first and foremost an amusement park of distinction. Denverites regard it almost as a civic institution. Theatergoers rank its showcase, America's oldest summer theatre, as one of the most outstanding in the nation. Through the years, crowds have danced to every top name orchestra in the country at the Trocodero Ballroom. Garden clubs and flower lovers admire the formal gardens, hanging baskets, entrance promenade, and geometric flower beds.

Elitch's is well within the city limits, and two city bus lines go right to the entrance on 38th Avenue. Inside the main gate, immediately to the right, is the miniature railroad station, with its

Puffer Belly Iron Horse. Its tracks circle the entire amusement area, and a train ride provides a better look around than even the Sky Ride does. To the left of the gate, in a meticulous garden setting, is the wonderful old merry-go-round, where the hand-carved horses seem prouder than most.

Elitch's two major roller coasters, including the famous Mister Twister, dominate the back of the park. All the old rides are there, including original bumper cars and the Spitfire with its high-flying planes on the giant swing. But there are new rides, too, like the Spider and the Calypso. There are only 10 major rides (plus 15 kiddie rides), but it seems as though there are a lot more when you are there.

Lagoon Amusement Park, midway between Salt Lake City and Ogden, Utah, was started with a bathing pavilion in 1896 by a former state governor, Simon Bamberger, to help his railroad. Today it has two dozen major rides, including one of the best roller coasters west of the Mississippi, a great fun house, an excellent penny arcade and shooting gallery, a million-gallon swimming pool, and one of the best-looking midways in America. The park is constantly being upgraded. The biggest recent revamp was the $250,000 improvement program in 1972, with five new rides added and others relocated.

Lagoon Park is famous for its annual Easter egg hunts, Saturday night rodeos, and its Opera House Square. This authentic reconstruction has an ice cream parlour, gaslight sandwich shop, sweet shop, and the opera house where big-time musicals as well as serious plays are staged in association with the drama department of the University of Utah.

Biggest of all traditional amusement parks in the West is Queen's Park in Long Beach, California, with 31 major rides, dozens of games, 3 separate penny arcades, 3 shooting galleries, and 5 full-scale restaurants.

An even better park is up the coast at Santa Cruz. Santa Cruz Beach has about half the rides Queen's Park has, but they are more fun. There's a particularly good Sky Ride, stretching along the shore of the ocean, not notably high but quite long and very well maintained. The Cave Train is a fake steam train, powered,

unfortunately, by a gasoline engine. Otherwise it's a delight on a
hot day. A section of its track goes under the kiddieland, and the
noise is terrific. Santa Cruz also has the Giant Dipper, one of the
last real roller coasters left on the West Coast.

Another good but small park in California is the Balboa Fun
Zone. Ray Olson keeps his little park sparkling, and the ocean surf
is better north of Los Angeles than south of it, as at Long Beach
where sometimes no swimming at all is allowed. The Balboa Fun
Zone also serves a particularly good hot dog.

In San Diego, Belmont Amusement Park used to be called
Mission Beach Amusement Park until the famous old Mission
Beach Ballroom was torn down. The biggest name bands in the
country used to enthrall thousands there during the big band era,
but this white elephant was mercifully razed in 1958, after having
been dark for years. There's a new dance pavilion now, and it is
surprisingly well attended with some people coming from
hundreds of miles away, particularly for the Friday night square
dances.

The park was also famous for bathing beauty contests and in-
stituted talent qualifications when the rest of the country was still
content just to look at 'em. Today's park coordinator, Jaynie
Baker, promotes more successful pageants of all kinds than anyone else. She keeps the park operating at full blast not only from
June through Labor Day but also during Christmas and Easter
school vacations.

Belmont Park has an exceptionally wide sandy beach, which
is patronized almost as heavily as its midway—one of the country's
busiest. Shorty, who at the age of 85 runs the Roll Down game, is
acknowledged as the best hustler of a buck on the midway. He's
been with the park since it opened in 1923. Lil, the game boss, has
been at Belmont since 1937. The Bat-A-Ball operator and his wife,
who operates the Rifle Range, have been around since the 1940s,
and so have the folks who run the cotton candy concession. All
wonderful people.

Some of Belmont's rides are almost historic. The merry-go-
round was brought to the park from Europe in 1923. The roller

The beach at Belmont Park in San Diego is almost as heavily patronized as its midway.

Lagoon Amusement Park near Salt Lake City maintains some of the most beautiful grounds in the state.

The Sky Glider at Seaside Park in Santa Cruz has long been a favorite of the patrons.

Lagoon Amusement Park began as a bathing pavilion in 1896 to encourage the use of the railroad.

coaster was built in 1925. The Scrambler, Monster, Ferris wheel, Skooters, Roll-o-Plane, and Pretzel rides were all in the park when World War II ended—and all are in good shape today and operating daily.

Appropriately enough, the only merry-go-round in the entire state of Nevada is in the front yard of a Las Vegas gambling joint called Circus Circus. This establishment also has a good bumper car layout and a kind of midway full of hanky-panks on the balcony that rings the casino floor. Circus Circus also has two shooting galleries, a penny arcade, Skee Ball and Fascination Halls, and pinball machines. And at the mechanical greyhound race you can win more than a Kewpie doll.

PARKS IN THE WESTERN STATES

WASHINGTON

★★Seattle—Fun Forest Amusement Park. Features miniature golf.

★★Tacoma—Funland Park. Features picnic facilities.

★★★Federal Way—Touray and Santafair. Features fun house, auditorium, children's theater, ballroom, ice rink, miniature golf, zoo, athletic field, picnic facilities, orchestras, name bands, vaudeville, fireworks, free acts. Operated in conjunction with theme park.

★★Redondo—Redondo Beach Park. Features beach, boating, marina, salmon fishing, picnic facilities.

IDAHO

★★Coeur d'Alene—Barber's Coast. Features beach, rowboat and canoe rentals, picnic facilities, free acts.

★★★Pocatello—Pleasureland Amusement Park. Features zoo, athletic field, picnic facilities.

★★Idaho Falls—Tauthaus Park. Features zoo, miniature golf, athletic field, picnic facilities, orchestras, free acts, fireworks.

★Boise—Julia Davis Park. Features zoo, miniature golf, picnic facilities.

WYOMING

★★Cheyenne—Playland Amusement Park. Features cafe, miniature golf, picnic facilities, showboat on the lake.

OREGON

★★Portland—Oaks Amusement Park. Features roller rink, ballroom, picnic facilities, free acts, fireworks.

★★Seaside—Gayway Amusement Park. Features roller rink, swimming pool, beach, Go-Karts, fireworks.

CALIFORNIA

★★★★Long Beach—Queen's Park. Features fun house, ballroom, picnic facilities, orchestras, name bands, free acts, fireworks. Open year around.

★★★San Diego—Belmont Amusement Park. Features fun house, swimming pool, beach, miniature golf, theater, picnic facilities, vaudeville, fireworks.

★★★★Santa Cruz—Santa Cruz Beach. Features fun house, beach, ballroom, miniature golf, picnic facilities, orchestras, name bands, vaudeville, free acts, fireworks.

★★Bakersfield—Hart Memorial Park. Owned by Kern County. Features beach, zoo, canoe rentals, pony rides, athletic field, picnic facilities.

★Los Angeles—Beverly Park Playland. Features party facilities.

★Pismo Beach—Pismo Fun Zone. Features ballroom, name bands.

★★★Balboa—Balboa Fun Zone. Features spin art, picnic facilities.

★Hawthorne—Rockwell Kiddieland.

UTAH

★★★★Salt Lake City—Lagoon Amusement Park. Features fun house, theater, swimming pool, racetrack, miniature golf, athletic field, picnic facilities, free acts, fireworks.

★★Lehi—Saratoga Fun Park. Features pools, miniature golf, marina, picnic facilities, free acts.

★★Salt Lake City—Liberty Park. Features swimming pool, zoo, museum, botanical gardens, tennis, free movies and band concerts, athletic field, picnic facilities.

COLORADO

★★Denver—Lakeside Amusement Park. Features fun house, racetrack, picnic facilities, orchestras, name bands, fireworks.

★★★★Denver—Elitch's Gardens. Features ballroom, summer theater, miniature golf, athletic field, picnic facilities, big-time entertainers, orchestras, bands.

★Grand Junction—Guyton's Fun Park. Features Space Pillow, miniature golf, picnic facilities.

NEW MEXICO

★★Albuquerque—Uncle Cliff's Familyland U.S.A. Features miniature golf, athletic field, picnic facilities.

ALASKA

★Anchorage—Totem Town Amusement Park. Features ice rink, zoo, museum, refreshment stand, name bands, free acts, fireworks.

Part 5

THOSE OTHER PARKS

20: Kiddielands

MOST kiddielands today are kiddielands in name only. Oh, sure, there are plenty of kiddieland sections in amusement parks, but the kiddielands that once operated as independent establishments, with miniature rides for small children exclusively, are about gone. With nothing for the adults, they simply couldn't draw enough repeat business; there just weren't enough doting grandmothers.

Most of the kiddielands that did survive widened their markets by building rides that appealed to teen-agers and adults. Some grew into full-scale amusement parks while retaining the kiddieland name. Others developed specialties; for example, all eight of the rides at Sea View Playland in Dennisport, Massachusetts, are kiddie rides but the place also has 85 hanky-panks. The 11-kiddie-ride Playland at Ocean City, New Jersey, also has 100 games, a Walk-Thru, fun house, penny arcade, miniature golf, and a bathing beach, but only 2 major rides. Since no operation with less than a bare minimum of three major rides can be considered a traditional amusement park, the Ocean City Playland is listed in this kiddieland chapter.

Also listed for the same reason are kiddielands that operate as

Young visitors to Idlewild Park in Ligonier, Pennsylvania, are greeted by this giant clown.

What were once simple playgrounds for children (such as the one at Hershey Park in 1915) have now become more sophisticated to keep pace with the new generation.

adjuncts to swimming pools, beaches, zoos, museums, driving ranges, motels, campgrounds, and drive-in movies. There's even one kiddieland in Topeka, Kansas, that is operated by the local Dairy Freeze.

Should a park with more kiddie rides than major rides be considered a kiddieland? Not in this book it shouldn't. That formula for classifying would make even the great Elitch's Gardens a kiddieland; it has 15 kiddie rides and only 10 major rides—but they are major indeed. Denver is a great town for the kids because that city's other major park, Lakeside, has 16 kiddie rides in its kiddieland section. But in spite of these two parks in Denver, there's no independent kiddieland in the state.

The first kiddielands started out as ordinary playgrounds, like the one provided at Hersheypark in Pennsylvania. Many early kiddie rides were built on the premises during the winter off-season. The first factory-built kiddie rides, such as the tethered little 4-passenger boats that moved slowly around in a small tank, were often designed more for the amusement of the parents watching their kids than for the kids themselves.

When automobiles were still scarce, kids could get a kick out of tooling around on a controlled course in a low-speed, self-propelled vehicle, but even small children today are more sophisticated and want to ride on a Ferris wheel or roller coaster, even if it is miniature. Practically all of the bigger kiddielands now have a self-controlled Helicopter ride, which is also a pretty good *adult* ride. Many also have a petting and feeding zoo, and most are cleaner and more gaily designed than they used to be.

In number of rides, the biggest kiddielands covered in this chapter are Victor's Kiddieland in Los Angeles, California, and the Doodle Bug Kiddieland in Treverton, Pennsylvania, with 15 kiddie rides each. Lincoln Park Amusement Company in North Dartmouth, Massachusetts, has 25 kiddie rides, but it has in addition 24 major rides and everything else that goes into making a good traditional amusement park. There are at least a dozen such traditional parks, with each having more kiddie rides in their kiddieland sections than Victor's or the Doodle Bug have.

But even what those dozen parks have is small potatoes compared to some of the kiddielands in overseas amusement parks. Takarazuka Familyland in Hyogo, Japan, has 86 kiddie rides. Wonderland Amusement Park in Singapore and Newton's in Durban, South Africa, each have 80 kiddie rides. Newton's doesn't have any major rides, either, unless you count the Dodgem layout.

Probably the most famous European amusement park associated with children is Linnanmäki Amusement Park in Helsinki, Finland. It is *really* operated for children. It's a traditional amusement park with 18 major rides and only 6 kiddie rides—but it is virtually *owned* by children. The park was built for the benefit of war orphans in 1950 by a foundation made up of six leading children's charities. The orphans are all grown now, but Linnanmäki continues to raise money to help succeeding generations of needy children. Because all the profits go to kids (and the profits are substantial), it is one park where you are extra glad to spend money. Bo Ekelund, the park's manager, welcomes all children (and retired people) with free admission for the first two hours every Sunday and holiday. It's a good park, too, and has the highest roller coaster in Europe.

The closest thing the United States ever had to Linnanmäki's concept was the kiddieland in Cisco, Texas, operated by the American Legion—but it folded in 1972. Other sizeable kiddielands that went out of business in the early 1970s include Green Oaks Kiddieland, Oaklawn, Illinois, which had 15 kiddie rides; Silver Boot Amusements in Clear Lake, Iowa, and Belair Kiddy Park, Detroit, Michigan, with a dozen kiddie rides each; Highway Kiddieland, Independence, Missouri, with 11; and Aherns Playland, Stratford, Connecticut, 10.

If you want to take your tots to an authentic kiddieland, you'd better hurry.

KIDDIELANDS

ALABAMA

Birmingham—Fair Park Kiddieland. Part of amusement park

complex at the State Fairgrounds but operated as separate entity by city. Basically a children's zoo with picnic facilities.

Oxford—Oxford Lake Park. Owned by the town of Oxford. Features bowling, roller rink, swimming pool, athletic field, picnic facilities, miniature golf, boating, fishing.

Tuscumbia—Spring Park. Lessee is the town's Parks & Recreation Department. Features pool, picnic facilities, exhibits, free acts.

ARIZONA

Phoenix—Wagon Wheels Kiddieland. Features Super-Slide, Astrobounce, picnic facilities.

ARKANSAS

Hot Springs—I.Q. Zoo. Features trained animal shows, zoo.

CALIFORNIA

El Cajon—Holiday Ranch. Features pool, playground, picnic facilities.

Lodi—Micke Grove Park & Zoo. Features swimming pool, picnic facilities, Japanese rock garden, camellia garden, rose garden.

Los Angeles—Tinkertown Carnival.

Los Angeles—Victor's Kiddieland.

Oakland—Knowland Park. Relatively new.

COLORADO

Denver—Mile High Enterprises. Features athletic field, picnic facilities, marina, zoo.

Grand Junction—Guyton's Fun Park. Features miniature golf, picnic facilities.

CONNECTICUT

New Haven—Lighthouse Point Park. City owned. Features miniature golf, boat launching ramp, beach, picnic facilities, athletic field, fireworks.

Rockville—Jack's Amusement Park. Features picnic facilities, pony rides, miniature golf.

FLORIDA

Daytona Beach—Ocean Front Amusements. New on the boardwalk. Features beach.

Miami—Crandon Park. Features ocean beach, roller rink, picnic facilities, miniature train, ocean tram ride, marina, zoo.

GEORGIA

Atlanta—Broadview Kiddieland. Features miniature golf.

Carrollton—Tanner's Beach. Features Super-Slide, beach, dance pavilion, picnic facilities, miniature golf, motel apartments, cottages, trailer park, free acts.

HAWAII

Honolulu—Ala Moana Keiki Land.

ILLINOIS

Harvey—Art's Amusement Center. Features roller rink, athletic field, picnic facilities, bowling.

Morris—Goold Park. City owned. Features pool, picnic facilities.

Quincy—Kiddieland.

INDIANA

Crawfordsville—Milligan Park. City owned. Features swimming pool, miniature golf, museums, athletic field, picnic facilities.

Hammond—Wicker Park Merryland. Features pool, ballroom, athletic field, picnic facilities, driving range. Operated in conjunction with 18-hole regulation golf course.

South Bend—Playland. Features ice rink, miniature golf, driving range, zoo.

IOWA

Des Moines—Kiddy Town Park. Features picnic facilities.

Iowa City—City Park Pool. Features pool, athletic field, picnic facilities, ice rink, zoo, fireworks on the Fourth of July.

Storm Lake—Lakeside Boating & Bathing. Features pool, beach, ballroom, picnic facilities, orchestras, name bands.

KANSAS

Hutchinson—Clown Town Kiddieland. Features trampolines, picnic facilities, miniature golf.

LOUISIANA

Shreveport—Hamel's Park. Features picnic facilities, zoo.

MARYLAND

Charlestown—Charlestown Manor Beach. Features beach, boating, athletic field, water sports, picnic facilities.

Takoma Park—Kiddieland Park. Features picnic facilities.

MASSACHUSETTS

Dennisport—Sea View Playland. Features beach, miniature golf, water cycles, par 3 pitch and putt golf course.

Mendon—Southwick Wild Animal Farm. Features zoo with elephant rides, picnic facilities, free acts.

Palmer—Forest Lake Resort. Features beach, ballroom, picnic facilities, orchestras, name bands.

Topsfield—Joytown Park. Features zoo, athletic field, racetrack, picnic facilities, ballroom, vaudeville, free acts.

MICHIGAN

Beaulah—Crystal Park. Features miniature golf, picnic facilities.

Grayling—Bear Mountain Resort. Features skiing, ice skating, togogganing, swimming pool, athletic field, picnic facilities, steam train, stagecoach, stable horses, bear museum, name bands, orchestras.

Houghton Lake—Houghton Lake Amusement Park. Features miniature golf, baseball pitching machines.

Traverse City—Clinch Park. City owned. Features beach, miniature city, zoo, museum, marina, picnic facilities.

MINNESOTA

New Ulm—Sioux Trail Park. Features miniature golf, Go-Karts.

MISSOURI

Kansas City—Riverside Red-X Kiddieland. Features racetrack, fireworks.

Monett—Monett City Park. City owned. Features swimming pool, picnic facilities, athletic field for baseball, tennis, archery, standard golf course, fireworks.

St. Charles—Blanchette Park. City owned. Features swimming pool, ice rink, ballroom, athletic field, picnic facilities, free acts, fireworks.

NEW HAMPSHIRE

Alton Bay—Land Ho. Features beach, marina.

Hudson Center—Benson Wild Animal Farm. Features wild animal acts, elephant and pony rides, athletic field, picnic facilities.

Spofford—Wares Grove Beach. Features picnic facilities, beach, name bands. Operated in conjunction with drive-in theatre.

NEW JERSEY

Asbury Park—Operators Amusement Company.

Atlantic City—Steeplechase Pier. Features fun house.

Bridgeboro—Holiday Lake. Operated as part of big holiday resort. Features dance floors, rowboats, canoes, power boats, private beach, swimming pool, athletic field, picnic facilities, miniature golf, bicycle paths, name bands, orchestras, vaudeville.

Columbus—Columbus Amusement Park.

Keansburg—Kiddie Park.

Springfield—Fairyland Park.

NEW YORK

Baldwin—Nunley Amusement Corporation. Features miniature golf.

Bronx—Bronx Beach. Features pool, beach, ballroom, athletic field, picnic facilities, free acts, orchestras, contests.

Brooklyn—Ward's Kiddieland. Features fireworks.

Brooklyn—Ward's Kiddie Park. Features fireworks.

Catskill—Catskill Game Farm. Features zoo, picnic facilities.

Cuba—Olivecrest Park. Features beach, roller rink, ballroom, picnic facilities, orchestras, local bands, fireworks.

Elmira—Harris Hill Park. Features miniature golf, driving range, picnic facilities.

Gloversville—Anthony Acres Park. Features beach, picnic facilities.

Howard Beach—Playland Center.

Irving—Sunset Bay Park. Features beach, miniature golf, picnic facilities.

Kingston—D-D's Kiddie Land.

New Hyde Park—Garden Amusement Park.

Newtonville—Hoffman's Playland. Features miniature golf, operated in conjunction with double-deck driving range complete with a pro shop.

Oceanside—Kiddieland.

Phoenix—Paul Mattle's Riverview Park. Features ponies, free kiddie acts.

Sodus Point—Sodus Point Beach. Features beach, ballroom, picnic facilities, miniature golf, name bands, orchestras, free acts, fireworks.
Staten Island—South Beach. Features beach.

Wilson—Wonderland Storybook Park. Features displays, picnic facilities, miniature golf, zoo.

NORTH CAROLINA

Raleigh—Pullen & Chavis. Features swimming pool, athletic field, picnic facilities, zoo.

Wilmington–Greenfield Gardens and Kiddie Zoo. City owned. Features boat rides, zoo, picnic facilities.

NORTH DAKOTA

Sibley–Sibley Resort on North Lake Ashtabula. Features beach, roller rink, ballroom, marina, picnic facilities. Operated in conjunction with motel and trailer court.

OHIO

Akron–Crystal Lake Park. Features kiddie pool, beach, athletic fields, picnic facilities. Operated in conjunction with barn dances, fishing, boating, campground.

Brunswick–Sleepy Hollow. Features swimming pool, beach, ice rink, ballroom, athletic field, picnic facilities, miniature golf, driving range, rifle and pistol range, archery, orchestras, name bands, vaudeville, free acts. Rides and attractions being phased out.

Cincinnati–Plaza Playland.

Circleville–Goldcliff Park. Features swimming pool, roller rink, athletic field, picnic facilities, driving range.

Cleveland–Memphis Kiddiepark. Features picnic facilities, miniature golf.

East Liverpool–Lake Marwin. Features swimming pool, beach, ballroom, picnic facilities, miniature golf, driving range, water rides, boating, fishing, free acts.

Geneva-On-The-Lake–P.G.'s Playland. Features picnic facilities, campground.

Hamilton–Meadowbrook. Features swimming pool, athletic field, miniature golf, picnic facilities.

New Philadelphia—Tuscora Park. Features swimming pool, athletic field, picnic facilities, free acts, fireworks.

Rootstown—Hickory Hills Park. Features athletic field, picnic facilities, paddle boats, rock bands, free acts, fireworks.

Toledo—Pearson Park. Features picnic facilities, bicycle rentals, tennis courts, bridle paths.

OKLAHOMA

Lawton—Doe Doe Park. Features swimming pool, roller rink, picnic facilities, zoo, train ride.

OREGON

Junction City—Benton Lane Park. Features swimming pool, roller rink, Go-Karts, picnic facilities.

Portland—Portland Children's Zoo. Owned by Portland Zoological Society. Features exhibits, picnic facilities, miniature boat ride. Operated in conjunction with zoo, aquarium, Lunarworld, theater, children's petting zoo, pet care center.

PENNSYLVANIA

Haydentown—Rainbow Park. Features miniature golf, swimming pool, picnic facilities.

Muncy—Trout Pond Park. Features roller rink, theater, athletic field, picnic facilities, orchestras, free acts.

Snow Shoe—Snow Shoe Park. Features swimming pool, museum, athletic field, picnic facilities, free acts. Operated in conjunction with racetrack, camping trailer park.

Stroudsburg—Pocono Wild Animal Farm. Features tame animals in zoo, bird sanctuary, picnic facilities.

Trevorton—Doodle Bug Kiddieland. Features picnic facilities, miniature golf, toyland store, free acts.

SOUTH CAROLINA

Spartanburg—Cleveland Park. City owned. Features pool, athletic field, picnic facilities, playground. Run in conjunction with zoo, fishing lake, tennis courts, bike trail.

TENNESSEE

Memphis—Kiddie-Land.

Tiptonville—Edgewater Beach Resort. Features beach, picnic facilities, miniature golf. Operated in conjunction with motel and cottages, nature tours by water, fishing, water skiing, boat ramp.

TEXAS

Borger—Huber Park Pleasure Island. Features miniature golf.

Corpus Christi—K-9 Kiddieland.

Fort Worth—Casino Beach. Features beach, ballroom, miniature golf, picnic facilities, speedboats, orchestras, name bands.

Henderson—Lakeforest Park. City owned. Features pool, beach, athletic field, miniature golf, zoo, picnic facilities.

Houston—Peppermint Park.

Lubbock—Tiny Texan Kiddieland. Features zoo, picnic facilities, miniature golf, free acts.

San Antonio—Brackenridge Park. No kiddie rides as such yet in this relatively new operation, but it has a 3½-mile train ride, pony rides, paddle boats, miniature golf, stable horses, zoo, and Chinese sunken gardens.

San Antonio—The Kiddie Park. Features picnic facilities.

WASHINGTON

Bellevue—Kiddyland. Features picnic facilities.

Redondo—Kiddyland. New Operation.

Tacoma—Point Defiance Park. Features 50-foot Parker antique merry-go-round.

WEST VIRGINIA

Parkersburg—McGuffey Amusement Park.

WISCONSIN

Fish Creek—Thumb Fun. Features miniature golf, driving range.

Fond du Lac—Lakeside Park. City owned. Features athletic field, band concerts, boat races, picnic facilities, zoo, fireworks on the Fourth of July.

Hortonville—Larry's Country Club. Features swimming pool, beach, athletic field, picnic facilities, orchestras, name bands, vaudeville, fireworks.

Oconomowoc—Silver Lake Beach. Features water rides, beach, picnic facilities, boats, surfboards, water skiing, fireworks.

Racine—Horlick's Kiddieland. Features water cycles, picnic facilities, birthday party room.

21: Theme Parks

Quite a few amusement parks call themselves theme parks only because of the popular trend started by Disneyland. Oklahoma's Frontier City, for example, indeed started with gun fights and train robbers for live entertainment but now also has 16 major rides, 8 quite conventional kiddie rides, a couple of fun houses, and other traditional attractions. Another good example is Petticoat Junction in Florida, which has practically forgotten about any connection there might have been with the now defunct television show.

It really is too bad that Walt Disney couldn't patent his idea, because there are a lot of theme park operators today who have become millionaires because they took advantage of his idea, although there are also a few who have gone broke, such as Freedomland in New York. In fact, there are a good many leechlike businesses clustered around Anaheim also getting rich off the worldwide popularity of Disneyland. However, the Disney organization didn't repeat that mistake when it started the Florida operation; whereas the California park covers only sixty-some acres, the new Disney World in Orlando owns surrounding acreage twice as big as the entire island of Manhattan—43 square miles. So if you are going to spend money in hotels or restaurants while visiting the six separate theme parks in Disney World (Cinderella's Magic Kingdom; Frontierland; Adventureland; Liberty Square; Tomorrowland; Main Street, U.S.A.), you can just as well spend it in establishments owned by Disney World itself.

July 17, 1955, when Disneyland opened so spectacularly, is considered as important to the industry as July 4, 1776, is to the rest of the country. The skyrockets going off over the castle are familiar to just about everyone in the world who has access to a television set. Walt Disney spared no expense to make his park the best possible. His heirs have not only continued that policy but seemingly operate Disneyland as a shrine to him without caring how much money they spend (but the more they spend, the more they make). Disney World now represents a $400-million investment.

Theme parks can be big, big business. Major corporations now into the industry include ABC, CBS, Taft Broadcasting, Avco, MGM, Warner Brothers, Hercules, and Westinghouse. Other large firms have entered via the sponsorship route, such as Marathon Oil, Sherwin-Williams, and Coca Cola. Many big parks have gone public, too.

Also jumping on the Disney World bandwagon was Al Capp, the creator of the Li'l Abner comic strip, who figured that if one cartoonist could make a mint by building a theme park around Mickey Mouse, he could do the same thing with Mammy Yokum. His Dogpatch, U.S.A., in Arkansas, grew so big that it is now designated as a town by the post office—and has gobbled up more than $7 million in capital investments.

Then Six Flags Over Texas was built as a complex of six separate multimillion-dollar theme parks, each with a national theme for the six countries that have ruled that area in the state's history. Everything at Six Flags Over Texas is big, including the profits. The owners stretched the idea and built Six Flags Over Georgia, and the Atlanta park has everything, including the famous old merry-go-round from Chicago's Riverview Park. From there they subsequently stretched the idea even more and built Six Flags Over Mid-America. But they may have gotten carried away with the idea inasmuch as that park near St. Louis isn't doing too well.

Another complex with half a dozen separate theme parks is the $30-million Kings Island, north of Cincinnati. Although it is dominated by the 340-foot replica of the Eiffel Tower, setting off the International theme area, the most heavily patronized area is built around the Coney Island theme. One reason for this is that the brand-new roller coaster was claimed to be the largest and fastest in the world. But unlike the original Coney Island, Kings Island is surprisingly clean.

Opryland, nine miles east of Nashville, has only one theme— music, as interpreted by the Grand Old Opry radio and television singers, fiddlers, and guitar players. There are a few rides and a couple of pretty good miniature railroads, but the park is mainly for people who like audience-participation shows and who slap their knees when Minnie Pearl says, "HowdEEE!" The management takes pains to point out how different Opryland is from the Disneyland-type theme parks— "We don't have any cold figures here, animated or otherwise, and everything here is live." Presumably this includes the people dressed up as 9-foot cartoon characters walking around on the grounds, such as Frankie Fiddle, Yancy Banjo, and Jose Mandolin.

Some self-styled parks don't have any discernible themes at all, such as Magic Mountain in Valencia, California. There's an observation tower, monorail, and flume ride, all to be expected in a multimillion-dollar theme park, but what's magic about that? Astroworld in Houston, Texas, has an olio of modern sky rides, imitation Wild West storefronts, a seal pool, flat rides, theaters, and penny arcades. But it would take an astrologer to connect it all with an astronaut.

The theme parks that most shamelessly exploit a theme are some of the Dutch parks around Lancaster, Pennsylvania. Buildings that look like B-movie English castles made of cardboard and an imitation 1914 streetcar that runs on brand new truck tires have absolutely nothing in common with the Amish people who live in the area (and whom the tourists think they will see). Well, maybe Bible World in Florida is worse. Figures from the Bible, Christ included, are not only animated but are wired for sound, speaking with what sounds suspiciously like a New York accent.

Some theme parks do start small, especially the ones developed around a natural tourist attraction such as an unusual lake or a cavern. A good example is Silver Dollar City, in Missouri near the Arkansas state line. When Hugo and Mary Herschend decided to retire to their favorite vacation spot in the Ozarks, they looked around for a small business to augment their retirement income and found that Marvel Cave in Branson, Missouri, was available on a 99-year lease. They leased the cave, but Hugo died shortly thereafter. Mary and her sons Jack and Pete pitched in to build a little village after the fashion of the 1880 mining town that once stood on the same spot. They decided to give change in silver dollars and therefore named the operation Silver Dollar City.

A master wood-carver, Peter Engler, asked permission to set up shop and sell his wares to the tourists. He was such a success that other craftsmen were invited to open shops. Today 21 craftsmen, including basket weavers, chandlers, broom makers, sawyers, textile weavers, wheelwrights, blacksmiths, candy makers, glassblowers, caners, and quilters, have their products on display. There you can find the only remaining Conestoga wagon factory in the country.

Also there are street shows in the day and stage shows at night. The steam train is attacked by "robbers" on every trip, and there are tours through a flooded mine and a burning town. The Ozark River float is a trip that just barely misses an enormous whirlpool. The park now has six major rides, two Walk-Thrus, six refreshment stands, and three full-scale restaurants.

Mary Herschend, who still manages the park, does not hesitate to install new attractions or to rectify any mistakes, such as the removing of two fun houses that weren't in keeping with the original theme. The operation has grown to the point where the

No one who witnesses the fireworks at Disneyland can forget the sheer spectacle. (Photo © Walt Disney Productions)

On a mere 60-acre tract, Disneyland has recreated dozens of fantasy worlds. (Photo © Walt Disney Productions)

Houston's Astroworld operates 27 major rides and 10 kiddie rides.

Al Capp's Mammy Yokum comes alive for visitors to Dogpatch, U.S.A.

Six Gun Territory in Silver Springs,
Florida, stages hourly gunfights.

San Jose's Frontier Village gives its patrons a taste of
the Old West with its stagecoach rides.

Three of Magic Mountain's most popular features are the 384-foot Sky Tower, the ultramodern Metro monorail, and the chilling Log-Jammer.

At night Kings Island's Royal Fountain is a spectacular sight as more than 330 multicolored lights illuminate 10,000 gallons of water. At one end of the fountain is the 33-story replica of the Eiffel Tower.

U.S. post office has given Silver Dollar City its own zip code.

Pete Herschend now has a nearby operation of his own called Talking Rocks, with a cave town, caverns, exhibits, picnic facilities, and nature trails. No rides yet. But Pete only began in 1973.

A miniature train is almost mandatory in any self-respecting theme park. Monorails represent a major investment and therefore are only for the big parks. Some of the relatively small parks, such as Fort Dells in Wisconsin covering only a few acres, make do with observation towers. Most of the new roller coasters in theme parks are built low to the ground, but inasmuch as they do not have all the old-time wooden superstructure, they seem extra swift. A flume ride, combining the features of a roller coaster and a Chutes, can be found in practically any big theme park.

Just about all theme parks, if there's any body of water around, have at least one stern-driven paddle wheel riverboat of one kind of another and, probably, a "dangerous" jungle cruise with an actor shooting a plastic alligator or hippo on every trip. A stagecoach ride (often attacked by Indians) is always a feature attraction at any park with a western theme, as is the street shoot-out or bank robbery. The strolling musicians employed by theme parks far outnumber the musicians currently employed by the movies and television studios combined.

There are also an impressive number of porpoises, seals, and other educated animals working in theme parks, with most of the smartest from Animal Behavior Enterprises in Hot Springs, Arkansas. A.B.E. is now also operating the I.Q. Zoo in Hot Springs, as well as the new Animal Wonderland, which opened in 1973. Did you ever see a chicken dance to the lilting accompaniment of a piano-playing rabbit? That rabbit's only serious rival is that performing porker Pigerace at Opryland.

The variously named Santa Claus theme parks are expressly for small children, as are some of the Mother Goose and Fairyland parks. But from the Enchanted Forest to the Frontier Towns and to Disney World itself, there's a weird aura of fantasy aimed at adults, too. One big reason for the one-price policy is to foster that escapist feeling; once inside the gate, the patron is living in fantasy, completely shut off from the hectic world outside.

THEME PARKS

ALABAMA

Fort Payne—Canyon Land Park. Features spectaculars, beach, picnic facilities, vaudeville acts.

ARIZONA

Scottsdale—Rawhide Arizona. Features panning for gold, animated buildings, cookouts, antiques, craft shops, museum, picnic facilities, bands, free acts.

Tempe—Big Surf Park. Features world's biggest filtered swimming lagoon, ocean surfing, swimming, beer and wine stands.

Tempe—Legend City Frontier Funland. Features Frontierland, miniature golf.

Tucson—Old Tucson. Features Old West gunfights, street shows, western exhibits, museums, sound stage, open-air ballroom, picnic facilities.

ARKANSAS

Dogpatch—Dogpatch, U.S.A. Features portrayals of Al Capp comic strip characters, gravity house, name bands, free acts.

Hot Springs—Animal Wonderland. Features dolphin show, macaw show, petting zoo, animal exhibits, deer farm, aviary, picnic facilities.

CALIFORNIA

Anaheim—Disneyland. Features audio-animatronics (electronically animated 3-dimensional figures), top-name entertainers, bands, acts, variety shows, house-talent performances, parades, holiday celebrations.

Buena Park—Japanese Village. Features Japanese dancers, karate demonstrations, ethnic restaurant, performing animals (bears, dolphins, sea lions, imperial Japanese koi, macaws, and a whale), tame deer on grounds, animals to feed and pet (doves, dolphin, carp, bear cubs).

Buena Park—Knott's Berry Farm. Features ghost town, free shows.

Eureka—The Shipwreck. Features aquarium, seal pool, maritime museum, picnic facilities.

Felton—Roaring Camp. Features steam railroad, redwood grove, general store, fishing pond, wagon rides, picnic facilities.

Laguna Hills—Lion Country Safari. Features African wildlife preserve, zoo, exhibits, electronic shooting gallery, picnic facilities.

Newhall—Callahan's Old West. Features historical Old West shows, Boot Hill, Indian museum, burro rides, trails, barn dances, old-time movies, western shoot-outs, ice rink, miniature golf, picnic facilities, orchestras, vaudeville.

Oceanside—Pacific Holidayland. Features ocean water sports, archery, miniature golf, picnic facilities.

Palos Verdes Peninsula—Marineland of the Pacific. World's biggest collection of marine mammals and fish. Features Sky Tower, cruise boats, picnic facilities.

Romona—Buckboard Acres. Features old mine site, burros, horses, children's zoo, swimming pool, athletic field, picnic facilities, free acts.

Redwood City—Marine World. Features oceanarium, headline shows, exhibits, boat rides, picnic facilities.

San Bernardino—Santa's village. Features Santa's village, picnic facilities, free acts.

San Diego—Sea World. Features aquatic shows with trained performing animals, marine exhibits, picnic facilities, fireworks on special occasions.

San Francisco—Cliff House Properties. Features hall of memories with Tom Thumb's personal collection, the Last Supper, Musée Mécanique, antique museum, promenade deck, marine deck.

San Jose—Frontier Village. Features Indian Island, panning for gold, old-time movie theater, trout fishing, 1890 schoolhouse museum, petting and feeding zoo, picnic facilities, vaudeville, free acts.

Santa Cruz—Santa's Village. Features Santa Claus Land, puppet theater, picnic facilities, free acts.

Skyforest—Santa's Village. Features Santa and Mrs. Claus, puppet theater, zoo, picnic facilities, vaudeville, free acts.

Stockton—Pixie Woods. City owned. Features animal sets, zoo, theater with guest appearances of movie stars, exhibits, beach, marina, athletic field, picnic facilities, free acts.

Valencia—Magic Mountain. Features amphitheater, name bands, free acts, vaudeville.

COLORADO

Canon City—Buckskin Joe. Features authentic 1869 town, log structures, exhibits, museum, gunfights, street shows, fun house, picnic facilities.

North Pole—Santa's Workshop. Features artisan shops, roving animals, magic and puppet shows, archery range, picnic facilities.

CONNECTICUT

South Norwalk—Old MacDonald's Farm. Features exhibits, zoo, picnic facilities.

FLORIDA

Barnum City—Ringling Bros.–Barnum & Bailey Circus World. Park still under development in 1974.

Bonita Springs—Everglades Wonder Gardens. Features Florida wildlife park and tropical gardens.

Dania—Pirate's World. Features musical comedy productions, street entertainment, name bands, free acts, zoo, picnic facilities.

Daytona Beach—Marco Polo Park. Complex of oriental villages still under construction when author last visited site.

Dunnellon—Rainbow Springs. Features *Rainbow Queen* double-deck paddle boat cruise, Rainbow Raft adventure, rodeo show, swamp garden, animal park, monorail, underwater cruise, bird park, gardens, fireworks.

Fort Lauderdale—Ocean World. Features porpoise show, oceanarium, Space Needle, refreshment stand.

Lake Wales—Masterpiece Gardens. Features museum, exhibits, zoo, deer petting and feeding park, outdoor theater, nature trails, formal gardens, jungle train tour, picnic facilities.

Miami—Parrot Jungle. Features bird shows, exhibits.

Orlando—Bible World. Animated depictions from the Bible still under construction when author last visited site.

Orlando—Walt Disney World. Biggest-of-'em-all park part of complex of six theme parks with own supportive city.

Panama City—Petticoat Junction. Features depiction of characters from television show, Cannonball Railroad with antique steam locomotives, hourly stage performances, name bands, free acts, hourly gunfights, jungle cat training center, nature trail, stable horses, zoo, museum, fun houses, pool, beach, miniature golf, picnic facilities.

St. Augustine—Marineland of Florida. Features marine shows, exhibits, picnic facilities, orchestras.

St. Petersburg—Florida's Sunken Gardens. Features subtropical botanical gardens, thousands of animals and exotic plants, aviary, museum.

St. Petersburg—MGM's *Bounty* Exhibit. Owned by Metro-Goldwyn-Mayer. Replica of ship made famous in *Mutiny on the Bounty* movie.

Sarasota—Circus Hall of Fame. Features circus museum, exhibits, puppet shows, guided tours.

Silver Springs—Six Gun Territory. Features hourly gunfights, stage shows at Palace Saloon, hourly Indian dances, museum, restaurant, fun house, picnic facilities.

Tampa—Busch Gardens. Features guided tours.

Tampa—Fairyland Park. City owned. Features Bambi Land deer park, zoo.

Tampa—Treasureland. Features Sound & Light Theater, museum, picnic facilities.

Weeki Wachee—Weeki Wachee—Florida. Owned by American Broadcasting Company. Features river cruise, mermaid show, trained bird show.

West Panama City Beach—Magic World. Features animal show, jungle boat ride, beach, miniature golf, picnic facilities.

GEORGIA

Atlanta—Six Flags Over Georgia. Features shows with emphasis on Georgia history, zoo, fun house, shooting gallery, picnic facilities. Six theme parks in one: British Village, Confederate section, Spanish section, French section, Georgia section, U.S.A. section.

Stone Mountain—Georgia's Stone Mountain. 3,800-acre park surrounds world's biggest granite monolith. Massive sculptures of Civil War heroes carved on face of mountain, viewable from Sky Lift. Features steam train ride around mountain, riverboat, Game Ranch, antique auto and music museum, Civil War museum, carillon concerts, antebellum plantation, nature trails, stable horses, picnic facilities, 18-hole championship golf course

ILLINOIS

Aurora—Pioneer Park. Features simulated old-time farming community (schoolhouse, hatchery, general store, blacksmith shop), railroad museum, carriage museum, general museums, sensory gardens, zoo, picnic facilities, vaudeville, free acts, name bands, fireworks, orchestras.

Spring Grove—Fair-O-Lea Farm. Features surrey rides, archery range, swimming pool, fishing pond, picnic facilities.

Utica—Mother Goose Gardens. Features storybook characters, live animals, miniature golf.

INDIANA

Chesterton—Enchanted Forest. Features tame deer, children's feeding and petting zoo, picnic facilities. Operated in conjunction with full-scale amusement park.

North Webster—Dixie Playtime. Features racetrack, miniature golf, driving range, picnic facilities, fireworks.

Santa Claus—Santa Claus Land. Features toy museum, doll museum, Lincoln museum, wax museum, educated animals, zoo, campgrounds, 18-hole golf course, picnic facilities, beach, German bands, free acts.

KANSAS

Seneca—Fort Markley. Features Old West town (jail, livery stable, log cabin, fire station, old fort, live buffalo, covered wagons, museum, general store, land office), swimming pool, outdoor ballroom, golf range, theater, rifle range, campgrounds, picnic facilities, name bands, free acts.

Wichita—Historic Restorations. Features exhibits, museum, ballroom.

KENTUCKY

Benton—Kaintuck Territory. Features saloon show, simulated gunfights, steam train, stagecoach, steam tractor ride, horses and ponies, museum, theater, picnic facilities, fun house, orchestras, name bands, free acts.

Cave City—Guntown Mountain. Features exhibits.

Cave City—Vertigo, Inc. Features fun house, picnic facilities.

Louisville—Ghost Town on the River. Features shows, roller rink, picnic facilities.

Parkers Lake—Tombstone Junction.

LOUISIANA

Tallulah—Delta Village. Features storybook land, museum, petting farm, zoo, boat rides, train rides, fun houses, picnic facilities, free acts.

MARYLAND

Ellicott City—Enchanted Forest. Features picnic facilities.

Ocean City—Frontier Town. Features saloon shows, rodeo, Indian dancing, beach, marina, picnic facilities.

MASSACHUSETTS

Orleans—Cranberry Cove. Features fiberglass zoo, action archery, miniature golf, picnic facilities, free acts.

Wakefield—Pleasure Island. Professes to be a theme park, although no theme is discernible. Features fun house, zoo, athletic field, picnic facilities, orchestras, name bands, entertainment personalities, free acts.

MICHIGAN

Coloma—Deer Forest. Features hundreds of animals and birds, deer feeding areas, rainbow trout pool and stream, Story Book Lane, miniature train ride through Africa-land, Santa's Summer Home, picnic facilities.

Davison—Sherwood Forest. Features stagecoach rides, sleigh rides, stable horses, hayrides, fun house, beach, ballroom, athletic field, picnic facilities, name bands.

Holland—Dutch Village. Features Dutch dancing, wooden shoe carver, Dutch street organ, Dutch house and barn with live animals, "Bit of Old Holland" Walk-Thrus, color movies about the Netherlands.

Holland—Wooden Shoe Land. Features exhibits, children's zoo, free acts, fun houses, miniature racetrack, picnic facilities.

Irish Hills—Stagecoach Stop. Features 1890 general store, western shop, theater, museum, exhibits, picnic facilities, free acts.

Onstead—Frontier City. Features Grand Old Opry shows, street shoot-outs, gun shows, deer park, stables, souvenirs at the general store, picnic facilities, name bands.

MINNESOTA

Brainerd—Paul Bunyan Center. Features lumber camp (bunk house and cook shanty) 26-foot animated statue of Paul Bunyan, 15-foot statue of Babe the Blue Ox, curio shops, free acts, Tilted Fun House, miniature golf, picnic facilities.

Brainerd—Lumbertown, U.S.A. Features authentic historical buildings, steamboat, special railroad, free acts, fun house, swimming pool, beach, ballroom, driving range, penny arcade.

Jackson—Fort Belmont. Features reproduction of old fort (log chapel, sod house, flour mill, log cabins), museum, picnic facilities.

Marble—Fairyland Park. Features handmade scenes of fairytales and folktales, antique doll collection.

Park Rapids—Deer Town. Features deer and wildlife park, trout pond, stagecoach ride, 100-foot observation tower, picnic facilities.

MISSOURI

Clarksville—Clarksville Skylift. Features western town, Indian burial grounds, riverboat museum, Indian museum, historical museum, country store, trained animals, deer park, free acts, observation tower, fun house, dancing on weekends, picnic facilities, orchestras, dance bands, fireworks.

Eureka (St. Louis)—Six Flags Over Mid-America. Complex of six theme parks.

Silver Dollar City—Silver Dollar City. Features street shows, night stage shows, 1880 craft workshops, exhibits, cave.

Sullivan—Jesse James Territory. Features steam train, stagecoach, historical exhibits, free acts, small zoo, fee fishing, orchestras.

MONTANA

Helena—Frontier Town. Features western town, museum, bar and lounge.

Lolo—Mother Goose Land.

NEBRASKA

Minden—The Harold Warp Pioneer Village. Features buildings depicting The Story of America and How It Grew, motel.

NEVADA

Incline Village—Ponderosa Ranch. Features frontier town, Silver Dollar Saloon, Ponderosa Ranch house, stable horses, museum, zoo, barbecues, fun house, western combos.

NEW HAMPSHIRE

Glen—Story Land. Features storybook characters, exhibits, picnic facilities.

Jefferson—Santa's Village. Features Christmas scenes, Santa Claus and Elves, Gingerbread Forest, All Faith Church, free acts, fun houses, theater.

Jefferson—Six Gun City. Features western town, simulated hold-ups and gunfights, free acts.

Lincoln—Natureland Home of Noah's Ark and Animals. Features wildlife preserve, museum, free acts, zoo, picnic facilities.

NEW JERSEY

Hope—Land of Make-Believe. Features Santa Claus, fun house, picnic facilities.

Pleasantville—Story Land.

West Milford—Jungle Habitat. Owned by Warner Bros. Features wildlife preserve, amphitheatre, artifacts shops.

NEW YORK

Ausable Chasm—Ausable Chasm Recreation Center. Features nature study theme, swimming pool, Go-Karts, athletic field, picnic facilities.

Catskill—Carson City & Indian Village. Features western town, free acts, picnic facilities.

Grand Island—Fantasy Island. Features western shoot-outs,

circus show, puppets, zoo, fun house, miniature golf, picnic facilities, fireworks.

Hamburg—Storyland Amusement Park. Features zoo, exhibits, picnic facilities.

Lake George—Gaslight Village. Features period museum, silent movies, fun houses, free acts, bands, vaudeville.

Lake George—Magic Forest. Features Indian village, zoo, free acts, picnic facilities.

Lake George—Storytown U.S.A. Features Alice in Wonderland, nursery rhyme displays, jungle land, ghost town, zoo with live storybook animals, athletic field, picnic facilities.

Lake Placid—Home of 1,000 Animals. Features fur and game farm, zoo, gift and fur shop.

North Hudson—Frontier Town. Features rodeos, western and Indian acts, full-size train, stagecoaches, zoo, swimming pool, beach, picnic facilities, motel.

North Pole—Santa's Workshop. Features Christmas village, crafts, zoo, free acts, picnic facilities.

Upper Jay—Land of Make-Believe. Not much fantasy. Features cocktail lounge, free acts.

Wilson—Wonderland Storybook Park. Features displays, zoo, refreshment stand, miniature golf, picnic facilities.

NORTH CAROLINA

Banner Elk—The Land of Oz. Features Walk-Thru park based on Wizard of Oz, museum.

Blowing Rock—Tweetsie Railroad. Features excellent miniature train ride, fun houses, picnic facilities, free acts.

Cherokee—Santa's Land. Features Santa's village, cartoon theater, puppet theater.

Concord—Frye's Lake. Features railroad town, historical gold mine, panning for gold, zoo, swimming pool, beach, roller rink, miniature golf, Go-Karts, slot car racing, picnic facilities.

Franklin—Lost Mine Town. Features fun house, free acts.

Maggie Valley—Ghost Mountain. Features mountaineer town, mining town, western town, Indian village, museum, exhibits, simulated gunfights, saloon shows, country and western shows, chair lifts up mountain, fun house.

OHIO

Aurora—Sea World. Features aquatic theater (whale, dolphin, seal, and penguin shows), Japanese pearl diving, seal and dolphin pools, trout pond, exhibits, deer park, zoo, picnic facilities, fireworks.

Findlay—Ghost Town Museum Park. Features museum, petting zoo, craft shops, gunfights, orchestras, free acts.

Kings Mills—Kings Island. Entertainment complex comprised of six theme parks.

Lakeside—Fort Firelands Park. Features frontier village, frontier craftsmen, swimming pool, beach, museum, outdoor ballroom, marina, campground, stable horses, picnic facilities, name bands, free acts.

Middletown—Fantasy Farm. Features museum, exhibits, zoo, antique displays, picnic facilities, swimming pool, zoo, athletic field, free acts.

Sandusky—Frontier Trail at Cedar Point Amusement Park. Features shows, bands, name entertainment in amphitheater, saloon shows, mine ride, antique car rides. Buildings include Red Garter Saloon, old-time candy factory, woodworking shop, blacksmith shop, replica of Fort Sandusky, early farmyard with live animals, trading post, working gristmill, glassblowing shop, town hall and museum, frontier hotel, emporium, Golden Palace Saloon, chuck wagon, Last Chance Saloon.

Sandusky—Lagoon Deer Park. Features 300 animals, seal pool, zoo, stocked fishing lakes, picnic facilities.

OREGON

Lincoln City—Pixieland Park. Features opera house shows, free acts, vaudeville, steam train ride, paddle boats, horses and ponies, picnic facilities, trailer park.

Newport—Undersea Gardens. Features underwater aquarium.

PENNSYLVANIA

Asheville—Animal Safari & Game Preserve. Features drive-through game preserve with roaming animals, petting zoo.

Gettysburg—Fantasyland Storybook Gardens. Features fairytale characters, puppet and animal show, displays, magic theater, barnyard theater, picnic facilities.

Jamestown—Pymatuning Deer Park. Features kiddie zoo with educated animals, western town, mule train rides, miniature train ride.

Lancaster—Dutch Wonderland. Features exhibits, gardens, theater, wax museum, campgrounds.

Schellsburg—Storyland.

West Chester—Lenape Park. Its only theme is amusement. Features fun house, pool, canoe rentals, athletic field, picnic facilities, fireworks.

SOUTH CAROLINA

Myrtle Beach—Pirateland Adventure Park. Features musical revue, animal acts, puppet show, museum, exhibits, picnic facilities, beach.

South of the Border—Pedroland (formerly Confederateland, U.S.A.). Features swimming pool, harness racetrack, zoo, miniature golf, 9-hole pitch-n-putt golf course, tennis, athletic field, picnic facilities, fireworks, motel.

SOUTH DAKOTA

Rapid City—Rockerville Ghost Town. Features gold mine, general store, log cabin, museum, exhibits, stagecoach ride, vaudeville, fun house, picnic facilities.

TENNESSEE

Gatlinburg—Gatlinburg Sky Lift. Features Sky Ride, photo concession.

Gatlinburg—Hillbilly Golf. Features Sky Ride, miniature golf.

Gatlinburg—Magic World.

Gatlinburg—Swiss Towers.

Nashville—Opryland, U.S.A. Features musical shows with stars from Grand Old Opry television and radio shows (The Grand Old Opry will move to Opryland's 4,400-seat auditorium and television studio in 1974), country and western music, hillbilly music, Dixieland bands, 1-hour musical revues, saloon shows, performing animal shows, audience-participation shows, horse pageant, square dancing, modernistic roller coaster called the Timber Topper, Flume Zoom, Tin Lizzie auto rides, blacksmith shop, weaving shop, hand-carved wood shop, petting zoo, museum, sidewalk cafes, restaurants—everything live, no animation.

Pigeon Forge—Goldrush Junction. Owned by Cleveland Browns football team. Features saloon shows, tintype concession, western print shop, blacksmith shop, train ride, simulated Indian attacks, exhibits, small zoo, picnic facilities, swimming pool.

Pigeon Forge—Porpoise Island. Features dolphin and sea lion

shows, bird shows, Hawaiian stage show, gardens, deer park, petting zoo, picnic facilities.

Sweetwater—Lost Sea. Features picnic facilities.

TEXAS

Arlington—Six Flags Over Texas. Six theme parks in one. Features musical revue, grandstand show, saloon show, puppet show, old movies, museum, exhibits, zoo, simulated gunfights, strolling musicians, porpoise show, fun house, picnic facilities.

Brackettville—Alamo Village. Features western town with simulated gunfights, stagecoach and wagon rides, pony ring, trail rides, free acts.

Galveston—Fort Crocket. Features western theme.

Grand Prairie—Lion Country Safari. Features African wildlife preserve, petting zoo, picnic facilities, free acts.

Houston—Astroworld U.S.A. Features theaters, open stages, seal pool, petting zoo.

Madisonville—Yesteryear. Features Old West exhibits, museum, buffalo range, zoo (exotic animals), picnic facilities.

San Marcos—Wonder World. Features cave, deer park, train ride through wildlife park, observation tower, fun house, picnic facilities.

VERMONT

Bellows Falls—Streamtown U.S.A. Features steam train excursions, museum of steam railroadiana.

Putney—Santa's Land U.S.A. Features Santa's workshop, schoolhouse, animal forest, zoo, picnic facilities, fun house, miniature golf.

VIRGINIA

Woodbridge—Story Book Land. Features live storybook characters, baby animal farm, picnic facilities.

WASHINGTON

Federal Way—Santafair. Features historic park, Hudson Bay Cabin, Spacedome, ice show, Muckleshoot Village, auditorium, children's theater, zoo, fun house, ice rink, ballroom, miniature golf, athletic field, picnic facilities, orchestras, name bands, vaudeville, free acts, fireworks.

WISCONSIN

Eagle River—Pleasure Island. The only discernible theme is amusement itself. Features fun house, racetrack, miniature golf, zoo.

Milwaukee—Franklin Park. The only discernible theme is amusement itself. Features racetrack, miniature golf, driving range, picnic facilities.

Waupaca—Ponderosa. Features western village with street shows, Silver Dollar Saloon, miniature mechanical farm, antique display, kiddie farm.

Wisconsin Dells—Enchanted Forest and Prehistoric Land. The wooded grounds constitute a giant Walk-Thru.

Wisconsin Dells—Fort Dells. Features 335-foot totem tower, farm animals, picnic facilities, fun house, free acts.

Wisconsin Dells—Storybook Gardens. Features live characters and animals, puppet shows, dollhouse, toy shop, book house.

Appendix

RECENTLY DEFUNCT AMUSEMENT PARKS

ALABAMA

Phenix City—*Idle Hour Park*. Featured pool, roller rink, ballroom, bowling, zoo, boating, fishing, athletic field, picnic facilities, miniature golf, racetrack, free acts, fireworks.

ARIZONA

Phoenix—*Jungle Park*. Featured fun house, picnic facilities, zoo, vended kiddieland. Noted for birthday party specialties.

ARKANSAS

Hot Springs—*Whittington Park*. Featured roller rink, ballroom, miniature golf, picnic facilities. Famous for fireworks.

CALIFORNIA

Santa Monica—*Pacific Ocean Park*. Featured biggest assortment of rides any traditional park ever had, separate kiddieland, ballroom, picnic facilities, big-name bands and talent.

San Francisco—*Sutro's (Whitney's)*. Featured fun house, miniature golf, Fun-Tier Town.

Pico Rivera—*Stream Land Park*. Featured pony rides, athletic field, picnic facilities.

Los Angeles—*Valley Fun Fair* (also known as Mom & Pop's Kid- dieland). Featured free acts, vaudeville, fireworks.

Sacramento—*Detweiler's*. Featured picnic facilities.

LaMesa—*Wally Park Playland*. Featured pony rides, covered wagon rides for birthday parties.

Norwalk—*Masseth Amusements*.

CONNECTICUT
West Haven—*Savin Rock Park*. Featured kiddieland.

DELAWARE
New Castle—*Kiddie Towne*. Featured miniature golf, racetrack, picnic facilities. Famous for children's birthday parties.

FLORIDA
Fort Walton Beach—*Okaloosa Island Park*. Featured fun house, beach, outdoor ballroom, miniature golf, zoo, picnic facilities, orchestras, name bands, fireworks.

Miami—*Funland Park*. Featured fun house, free acts, fireworks.

Panama City Beach—*Long Beach Resort*. Featured beach, roller rink, miniature golf, zoo.

Miami—*Havlover Beach*. Featured athletic field, zoo, bathing beach, picnic facilities.

Sarasota—*Floridaland*. Featured porpoise show, ghost town, deer park, saloon show, variety acts, gardens, picnic facilities.

GEORGIA
Atlanta—*Lakewood Park*. Featured fun house, roller rink, picnic facili- ties, racetrack with a grandstand seating 6,000 people, free acts, fireworks.

Atlanta—*Funtown*. Featured dance pavilion, miniature golf, picnic facilities, free acts, fireworks.

Atlanta—*Storyland*. Featured Mother Goose theme gardens, gift and toy house, picnic facilities.

Macon—*Ragan's Park*. Featured pool, beach, roller rink, ballroom, picnic facilities.

IDAHO

Coeur d'Alene—*Playland Pier*. Featured lake.

ILLINOIS

Chicago—*Riverview Park*. Featured fun house, roller rink, miniature golf, picnic facilities. Fireworks on the Fourth of July were a tradition with Chicago mayors for many years.

Spring Valley—*Midway Park*. Featured picnic facilities.

Aurora—*Exposition Park*. Featured fun house, pool, rink, ballroom, athletic field, picnic facilities, full-scale racetrack, free acts, fireworks, orchestras, name bands, vaudeville.

Skokie—*Fun Fair*. Featured miniature golf, free acts, fireworks.

Bloomington—Fun Fair. Featured pool, beach, athletic fields, miniature golf, zoo, picnic facilities, concerts, free acts, fireworks.

Dundee—*Funland*. Featured frontier museum.

Fox River Grove—*Fox River Picnic Grove*. Featured beach, ballroom, athletic field, picnic facilities, cocktail lounge, boat launching and marina, orchestras, name bands.

Morton Grove—*Kiddieville*.

Oaklawn—*Green Oaks*.

South Elgin—*Fox Valley Park*. Featured animated storybook characters, antique buggies, miniature mountain with waterfall.

INDIANA

Indianapolis—*Riverside Amusement Park*. Featured fun house, tavern, ballroom, picnic facilities, orchestras, name bands, free acts, fireworks.

Evansville—*Yabroudy Park.* Featured miniature golf, athletic field, picnic facilities.

Gary—*Porter's Kiddieland.* Featured athletic field, small zoo, picnic facilities. Noted for birthday specials.

Vincennes—*Uncle John's Kiddieland.*

IOWA

Council Bluffs—*Playland Park.* Featured fun houses, racetrack, miniature golf, picnic facilities, orchestras, free acts, vaudeville, fireworks.

Clear Lake—*Silver Boot Amusement Park.* Featured roller rink, picnic facilities.

Cedar Rapids—*Cemar Amusement Center.* Featured roller rink, picnic facilities, free acts.

KANSAS

Wichita—*Sports Center.* Featured pool, roller rink, miniature golf, driving range, picnic facilities, name bands, free acts, fireworks.

Junction City—*Crains Rides.*

KENTUCKY

Louisville—*Fontaine Ferry park.* Featured fun houses, pool, beach, roller rink, ballroom, athletic field, picnic facilities, orchestras, name bands, free acts, fireworks.

Ross—*Riverview Playground.* Featured swimming pool, miniature golf, athletic field, picnic facilities, marina, orchestras, fireworks.

Louisville—*Kiddieland.* Featured miniature golf.

LOUISIANA

New Orleans—*Lincoln Beach.* Featured fun house, pool, beach, ballroom, picnic facilities, orchestras, name bands, vaudeville, free acts, fireworks.

MAINE

York Beach—*Animal Forest Park.* Featured fun houses, beach, athletic field, miniature golf, zoo, storyland, picnic facilities, vaudeville, fireworks, free acts.

MARYLAND

Glen Echo—*Glen Echo Park*. Featured fun house, basketball, Skee Ball, picnic facilities, vaudeville, rodeo, Indian dancing, circus acts, cancan show.

Tolchester—*Tolchester Park*. Featured hotel, beach, athletic field, miniature golf, picnic facilities.

Braddock Heights—*Braddock Heights Park*. Featured roller rink, ballroom, bowling, summer playhouse, zoo, picnic facilities.

Pasadena—*Cottage Grove Amusement Park*. Featured ballroom, athletic field, picnic facilities.

MICHIGAN

St. Joseph—*Silver Beach Amusement Park*. Featured fun house, ballroom, beach, picnic facilities.

Bay City—*Wenona Beach*. Featured roller rink, ballroom, athletic field, picnic facilities.

Kalamazoo—*Kiddieland Park*. Featured picnic facilities, miniature golf, pony rides.

Southgate—*Wonderland Park*.

Birch Run—*Pine Ridge Amusement Park*. Featured miniature golf, zoo, picnic facilities, country music band on Sundays, with talent from the Grand Ole Opry.

Dearborn Heights—*Motor City Park*.

Utica—*Utica Amusement Park*. Featured beach, ballroom, miniature golf, athletic field, picnic facilities, free acts, orchestras, fireworks.

Manitou Beach—*Lakeview Park*. Featured beach, roller rink, ice rink, athletic field, miniature golf, ski shows, boat rides, ballroom, picnic facilities, orchestras, name bands, fireworks.

MINNESOTA

Minneapolis—*Queen Anne Kiddieland*. Featured picnic facilities.

MISSOURI

Independence—*Highway Kiddieland*. Featured fun house.

Branson—*Marvel Cave Park*. Featured fun houses, free acts.

St. Louis—*Gay 90's*. Featured huge penny arcade, collection of musical machines all in working order.

NEBRASKA

Omaha—*Carter Lake Pleasure Pier*. Featured beach, ballroom, dance pavilion, miniature golf, athletic field, picnic facilities, banquet and picnic catering, orchestras, name bands, fireworks.

Norfolk—*Sunshine Park*. Featured miniature golf. Oswald Reiche, the owner, had his own dog act.

NEW JERSEY

Palisade—*Palisades Amusement Park*. Featured fun house, pool, beach, baseball batting range, archery, miniature golf, basketball, picnic facilities, orchestras, name bands, vaudeville acts.

Maplewood-Irvington—*Olympic Park*. Featured fun house, pool, beach, roller rink, miniature golf, athletic field, picnic facilities, free acts, fireworks.

Seaside Heights—*Funtown U.S.A.* Featured fun house.

Asbury Park—*Wesley Amusement Park*. Featured motorboats, showboat.

Atlantic City—*Funcade*.

Bayonne—*Uncle Milty's*.

NEW YORK

Bronx—*Freedomland*. Featured fun house, institutional exhibits, outdoor ballroom, athletic field, miniature golf, theater, zoo, picnic facilities, orchestras, name bands, vaudeville, fireworks, Roman chariot races.

Cheektowaga—*Carrousel Gardens*. Featured fun houses, beach, ballroom, theater, miniature golf, athletic field, picnic facilities, summer stock theater, orchestras, name bands, fireworks.

Auburn—*Owasco Lake Park*. Featured ballroom, miniature golf, athletic field, picnic facilities, free acts, fireworks.

Hamburg—*Funtown*. Featured fun house, ice rink, ballroom, swimming pool, athletic field, picnic facilities, miniature golf, zoo.

Sylvan Beach—*Sylvan Beach Midway.* Featured beach, boating, picnic facilities, free acts, fireworks.

Douglaston, Long Island—*Kiddy City.* Featured archery range, miniature golf.

Flushing—*Fun Fair Park.* Featured miniature golf.

Elmhurst—*Fairyland Park.* Featured miniature golf, free acts.

Corfu—*Boulder Amusement Park.* Featured picnic facilities.

Angola—*Lalle's New Amusement Park.* Featured fun house, picnic facilities, motel, orchestras.

Niagara Falls—*Midway Beach Park.* Featured fun house, beach, ballroom, athletic field, racetrack, picnic facilities, orchestras, name bands, vaudeville, fireworks, boat races, regattas, beauty contests.

Huntington—*Fairyland.* Featured miniature golf.

Salamanca—*Fentier Village* (That's right, *Fentier*, not Frontier—it was owned by Ned Fenton). Featured fun houses, ballroom, picnic facilities.

Peekskill—*Buy-Rite Kiddieland.* Featured miniature golf, picnic facilities.

New York—*Fordham's Playland.* Featured miniature golf.

NORTH CAROLINA

Franklin—*Gold City.* Featured fun house, gunfights, stage shows, gold panning, stagecoach, burros, magic carpet slide. Not gone entirely, but owner Charley Tombras sold out to Don Vernine, who now operates just rides, fun house, refreshment stands, and some of the shops.

Winston-Salem—*Reynolds Memorial Park.* Featured pool, roller rink, athletic field, picnic facilities, full-scale golf course, clown acts, fireworks.

OHIO

Cleveland—*Euclid Beach Park.* Featured fun house, ballroom, athletic field, miniature golf, picnic facilities. Famous for fireworks.

Cincinnati—*Coney Island*. Featured pool, ballroom, miniature golf, athletic field, picnic facilities, orchestras, name bands, free acts, fireworks.

Cincinnati—*Kissel Brothers Amusement Park*. Featured fun house, ballroom, athletic field, miniature golf, zoo, picnic facilities, free acts, fireworks.

Russells Point—*Sandy Beach Park*. Featured fun houses, pool, beach, roller rink, ballroom, athletic field, miniature golf, picnic facilities.

Craig Beach Village—*Craig Beach Park*. Featured beach, ballroom, boats, archery, picnic facilities. Noted for fireworks.

Cincinnati—*Playland*. Featured picnic facilities.

Toledo—*Wee Tee Amusements*. Featured miniature golf.

Akron—*Sandy Beach Park*. Featured beach, picnic facilities, marina with complete sales and service.

Hamilton—*Plaza Kiddieland*.

OKLAHOMA

Oklahoma City—*Frontier City U.S.A.* Featured fun houses, Indian Village, dancers, train robbers, gunfights, zoo, nationally known celebrities, radio and television stars, free acts, fireworks.

Oklahoma City—*Wedgewood Village*. Featured bowling, pool, ballroom, Go-Karts track, miniature golf, driving range, picnic facilities, orchestras, fireworks.

Lonewolf—*Craterville Amusement Park*. Featured fun house, zoo, race-track, stock car races, thrill shows, rodeos.

OREGON

Portland—*Jantzen Beach Park*. Featured fun house, pool, bowling alley, athletic field, racetrack, picnic field, racetrack, picnic facilities. Noted for fireworks displays.

PENNSYLVANIA

Denver—*Make-Believe World*. Featured fun house, zoo, Frontier World, Buccaneer World, Space World, Santa's World, Children's World, Animal World.

Sunbury—*Rolling Green Park.* Featured fun house, miniature golf, swimming pool, ballroom, athletic field, Strato-Slide, picnic pavilions.

McKeesport—*Rainbow Gardens.* Featured fun house, pool, beach, roller rink, miniature golf, athletic field, picnic facilities, drive-in theater.

Hanover—*Forest Park.* Featured roller rink, ballroom, athletic field, picnic facilities, orchestras, fireworks, vaudeville.

Harvey's Lake—*Hanson's Amusement Park.* Featured beach, ballroom, picnic facilities.

Lancaster—*Rocky Springs Park.* Featured fun house, swimming pool, roller rink, ballroom, athletic field, racetrack, picnic facilities.

Wilkes-Barre—*Sans Souci Park.* Featured pool, ballroom, athletic field, picnic facilities, orchestras, name bands.

Drums—*Angela Park.* Featured swimming pool, miniature golf, beach, ballroom, athletic field, picnic facilities, orchestras, name bands, free acts, fireworks.

Butztown—*Willow Amusement Park.* Featured swimming pool, ballroom, athletic field, picnic facilities.

Middletown—*Swatara Park.* Featured ballroom, athletic field, picnic facilities, orchestras, name bands, free acts, fireworks.

Morton—*Playland Park.* Featured miniature golf, free clown acts.

Lake Ariel—*Lake Ariel Park.* Featured beach, ice rink, athletic field, picnic facilities, free acts, fireworks.

Walnutport—*Edgemont Park.* Featured roller rink, picnic facilities, vaudeville, fireworks.

Butler—*Old MacDonald's Farm.* Featured Fun Barn, farm produce stand, general store, zoo, dancing, evening parties.

Lemont Furnace—*Shady Grove Park.* Featured swimming pool, roller rink, ballroom, picnic facilities.

Union City—*Canadohta Lake Park.* Featured miniature golf, driving range, picnic facilities, orchestras, free acts, fireworks.

Hawthorn—*American Legion Park.* Featured swimming pool, athletic field, roller rink, picnic facilities.

Hegins—*Dell Lake Park*. Featured pool, picnic facilities.

Johnstown—*Billow's Amusement Park*. Featured bowling, picnic facilities.

Apollo—*Kiski Valley Park*. Featured beach, picnic facilities.

Butler—*Circustown, U.S.A.* Featured pony rides, zoo, animal farm, museum, boating, athletic field, picnic facilities.

Pittsburgh—*Maple Grove Park*. Featured swimming pool, roller rink, ballroom, picnic facilities.

TENNESSEE

Nashville—*Frontier Town*. Featured western town, cancan saloon, stagecoach, gunfights, train, picnic facilities.

TEXAS

Houston—*Playland Park*. Featured fun house, racetrack, picnic facilities.

El Paso—*Washington Park*. Featured pool, roller rink, miniature golf, zoo, athletic field, picnic facilities. Noted for fireworks displays.

Waco—*Westview Playland*. Featured air-conditioned roller rink, miniature golf, baseball batting concession, trampoline center, Go-Karts.

WASHINGTON

Spokane—*Natatorium Park*. Featured ballroom, zoo, picnic facilities, orchestras, name bands, vaudeville, free acts, fireworks.

WEST VIRGINIA

Chester—*Rock Springs Park*. Featured ballroom, athletic field, picnic facilities.

INDEX